Alberto C. Carpiceci

POMPEII

2000 years ago and today

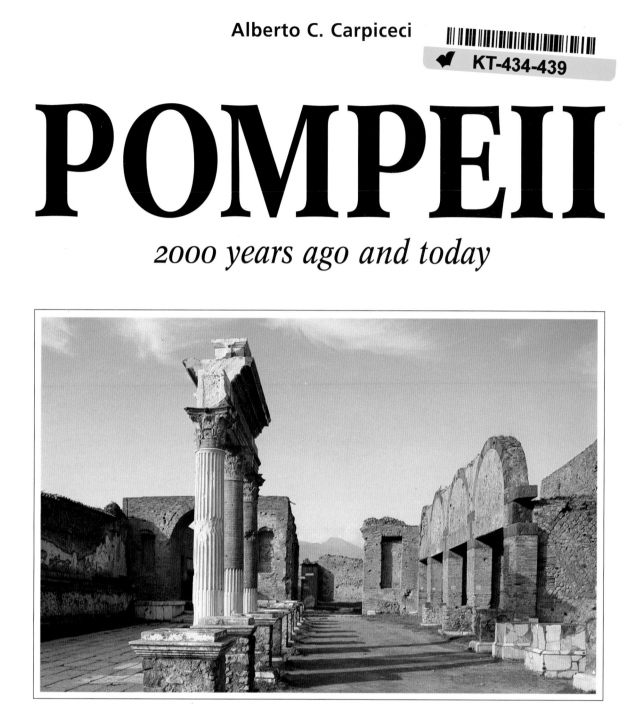

150 color photographs
36 reconstructions and drawings
Map of the excavations

BONECHI EDIZIONI "IL TURISMO"

This study aims at giving a living impression of Pompeii as it was two thousand years ago. We have therefore tried to include, in the form we hope is most useful, everything that could help bring us closer to this people who lived so many centuries before us. Theirs was a society basically not very different from our own, but they had a more active sense of participation in life and a more sensitive feeling for nature, which surrounded them constantly.

Because of its exceptional conditions, Pompeii offers us great possibilities for·recreating the life of its inhabitants through the innumerable remains discovered there. To assist us in imagining the city as it was, we have included reconstructions and drawings which give an idea of its basic elements, such as the house, the villa, the public building, the street and a general view of the city centres as they might have been in the Ist century. Even the information in this guide is not enough to see all the city thoroughly, a project which would require at least two or three days if it is not to prove tiring and confusing. But to get to know Pompeii, it is enough to make a careful tour of its most important and fascinating sites, especially those which each visitor may personally find most congenial and interesting. For this reason, the features considered most important have been indicated by capital letters in the text, and each visitor can choose those which best suit his own inclinations and arrange his itinerary accordingly. However, it should always be remembered that this marvellous visit to the past must be made on foot.

In our guide, each site as described has a number which is also shown on the map, separate from the text, of Pompeii. The name of each monument is also followed by the number of the region (Reg.), the block or " insula " (Ins.) and the entrance number, as they appear on the site itself. In case of doubt, or to ask for closed doors or gates to sites to be opened, the visitor should seek the nearest custodian. For those who have a limited amount of time, on the map outside the text we have given three suggested itineraries which occupy only a few hours.

Reconstruction of the terrible eruption of Vesuvius in 79 A.D.
which destroyed not only Pompeii but all forms of life from Herculaneum to Stabiae.

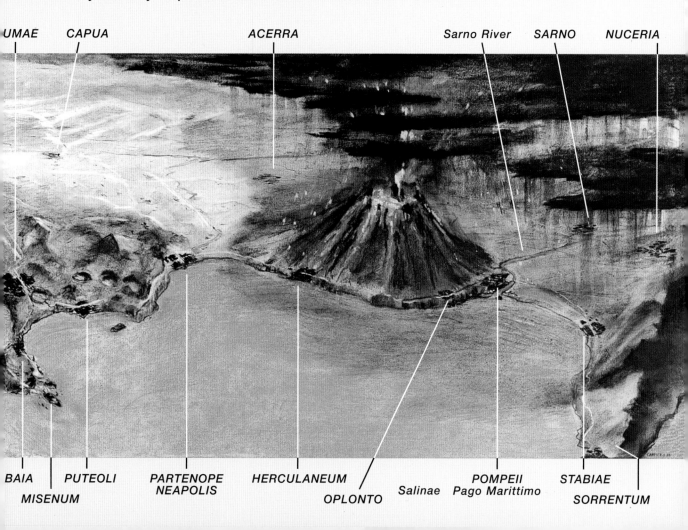

UMAE   CAPUA   ACERRA   Sarno River   SARNO   NUCERIA

BAIA   PUTEOLI   PARTENOPE   HERCULANEUM   POMPEII   STABIAE
NEAPOLIS
MISENUM   OPLONTO   Salinae   Pago Marittimo   SORRENTUM

ORIGINS AND HISTORY. The origins of Pompeii are as ancient as those of Rome: the first settlement was founded there and given its name in the 8th century B.C. by the " gens pompeiana ", who belonged to the Osci, one of the oldest of the Italic peoples. Since it lay on the only route between north and south and between the sea and the fertile valleys of the hinterland, Pompeii rapidly became an important road junction and port, attracting the attention of the powerful states around it.

The first of these to subjugate Pompeii was the Greek state of Cumae. The Greeks were ousted between 525 and 474 B.C. by the Etruscans, at the height of their expansion. Then towards the end of the fifth century B.C. the city was taken over by the Samnites during their powerful outward thrust from the Appennine zone of Isernia towards the Tyrrhenian Sea.

In 310 B.C. the Samnites were defeated in turn by the Romans, and Pompeii became part of the emerging Roman state. But it joined the Italic revolt, the Social War against Rome, and was crushed by Sulla: although the city was saved from destruction it lost all trace of autonomy, becoming a colony called « Colonia Veneria Cornelia P. » in honour of its conqueror (L. Cornelius Sulla). These six centuries passed and each of Pompeii's various rulers left behind their customs and art in the city, especially the Samnites, of whom important traces remained in Pompeii's buildings and art even after four centuries of progressive Romanization.

FIRST DISASTER AND POMPEII'S DESTRUCTION. Despite all these political upheavals, Pompeii's development continued, and from a modest farming town it became an important industrial and trading centre. The first great disaster to hit it was the terrible earthquake in 62 A.D., which left the city no more than a heap of rubble. But the Pompeians who survived set about rebuilding, and their energy soon restored the city's industrial and commercial activities as it rose again from the ruins. They were in the process of completing and extending its temples when the second disaster struck, and this one was the end for Pompeii: Vesuvius, which for centuries had been considered extinct and was thus covered with vineyards, farmhouses and luxurious villas, on 24 August (24 November according to some scholars) 79 A.D., shortly after midday, suddenly returned to life and erupted with savage violence.

From Misenum, Pliny the Younger witnessed the fearful spectacle, « the appearance and form of which no tree better represents than the pine ». He gives a striking description of it and of the final hours and tragic end of his uncle, Pliny the Elder, who, attracted partly by scientific interest, approached by ship to observe the frightening phenomenon and died as he sought to help and cheer his friend Pomponianus. Flames from the volcano soared high into the sky, but an immense black cloud soon rose above them, blacking out the sun. Volcanic matter, lapilli and red-hot scoriae, rained down on Pompeii. Walls and roofs crumbled, then ashes mixed with water fell until all forms of life were extinguished. Darkness reigned and the scene was made even more apocalyptic by lightning, earthquakes and tidal waves. The few survivors who sought to escape in the direction of Stabiae or Nuceria were overtaken and killed by the poison gases which spread everywhere. The inferno continued for three days, and then all was silence. A layer of death, from five to six metres (15-20 feet) deep, covered the area from Herculaneum to Stabiae.

POMPEII REAWAKES AFTER NINETEEN CENTURIES. Vesuvius was to remain active for many centuries, up until our own time; the other cities around it were rebuilt, more or less on the same sites as before, but Pompeii remained buried for nearly two thousand years. People feared the site, as if a terrible spell had been cast over it. Looters and treasure-hunters carried off what they could from the ruins near the surface, but then Pompeii was forgotten and all trace of it lost. One thousand six hundred years passed before the first ruins were properly uncovered, and another one hundred and fifty years before the city could be said to have been rediscovered.

The excavations begun under the Bourbon rulers of Naples served only to rob the city of its most interesting works of art, on which the creation of the great National Museum of Naples was based. Further hurried excavations at the beginning of the 19th century brought to light the Forum, but it was left as little more than a pile of ruins.

Pompeii's exceptional state of preservation was partly due to Giuseppe Fiorelli, who began work in 1860. He carried out systematic and intelligent excavations and was the first to obtain impressions by pouring plaster of Paris into the spaces left by the organic substances which had decomposed after the volcanic ashes solidified; by this method we have preserved the exact forms of the bodies of men and animals, plants and other objects reduced to dust one thousand nine hundred years ago.

In the decades which followed, the work of preservation and restoration reached much higher levels, and since 1909, under Vittorio Spinazzola, buildings have been preserved from roof to foundations and every object hidden under the volcanic ash for so many centuries has been recovered. Increasingly precise excavation work is continuing in the part of the city which remains to be discovered (about one-quarter of it), and Pompeii seems almost to have returned to life, awakening after a sleep lasting nineteen centuries, though in place of its hard-working inhabitants of ancient times are the tourists of today, on their hasty visits.

On this and on the following page:
view of Mount Vesuvius.

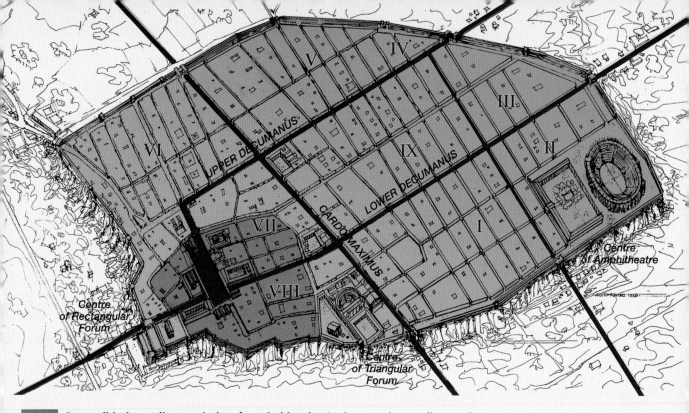

Pompeii in its earliest period as founded by the Osci, an ancient Italic people.
Development of the city under the Greeks and the Etruscans.
Maximum extension of the city reached already under the Samnites.

THE CITY. Pompeii was built at the end of an ancient flow of lava 40 metres (130 feet) above sea level, on the mouth of the River Sarno, then much closer to the city. The first settlement, a farming village, was in the area around the Forum. The city was restored and extended by the Greeks (and for a short time also by the Etruscans), who began to build a new forum, the Triangular Forum, and continued road-building in the city in a more or less orderly way. The city's maximum expansion was under the Samnites, so that when the Romans arrived its massive walls had already been built, extending for three kilometres (two miles) and enclosing an urban area occupying 66 hectares (165 acres). Pompeii under the Samnites was already a large city at the end of the 4th century B.C., larger than the other nearby centres and the still modest town of Neapolis, now Naples. It was destined to grow larger than Cumae, but when it came under Roman rule its expansion stopped. Thus in the 350 years which followed the shape of the city did not alter: the continual process of renovation which went on remained inside the confines of the Samnite city.

The changes which Imperial Rome made to Pompeii involved mainly reorganization and renovation: high footpaths were built (with crossings on big stones because the streets had no drainage); traffic was controlled by rational planning involving the creation of zones reserved for pedestrians (for example, the Forum) and zones with limited access (for example, the Amphitheatre); the public baths were enlarged and three baths centres opened at points where the demand was greatest; and the city's civic centres were better equipped to fulfil three distinct social functions. From the time of the Samnites the city had been divided into nine parts by two main streets running lengthways (decumani) and two others crossing them (cardines); each of these areas had its own festivals, electoral programmes and economic and commercial characteristics. Near the city gates and around the Forum there were inns (« hospitia ») and stables (« stabula »), while along the main streets there were many taverns (« cauponae ») and the forerunners of our cafés (« thermopolia »).

Each building had its own water tank, filled by rainwater from the roof, and Rome built a deviation of the Augustan acqueduct of Serino from which water was supplied to the baths, public fountains and richest dwellings. There were few sewers and almost all of them were connected to the public latrines, while private houses had individual sewage pits. Pompeii had about 20,000 inhabitants, including numerous merchants, freedmen and slaves (of Greek and Asiatic origin or from around Rome) and less numerous noble families (of Samnite origin or people who had moved to Pompeii from Rome).

The merchant class in Pompeii continued to grow, to such an extent that the old residential buildings began to disappear, taken over or replaced by new shops or industries. The merchants who became rich converted the austere Samnite houses into opulent residences, often going so far as to unite two or three of the older houses. During the city's last period, when the "Peace of Augustus" made any defensive measures superfluous, buildings were erected on parts of the city walls or even outside them.

Pompeii had two governors ("duumviri"), who were appointed for five years. Also part of the government were the two "aediles", who were in charge of public health and public entertainment, of the market and food provisions for the city, and the supreme council ("ordo decurionum"), consisting of a hundred citizens of Pompeii elected because of special merits.

All important news regarding the life of the city, such as elections, public entertainment and advertisements, were written or drawn by expert "scriptores" on the walls of the buildings.

Much more numerous are the graffiti on Pompeii's walls: they are a sort of endless notebook in which everybody wrote - shopkeepers, lovers, students, sporting fans, the tourists of those times, and even swindlers and procurers. In this enormous number of rapid jottings, hundreds of people seem still to speak to us about the ordinary problems of daily life in the language of 2000 years ago.

THE IDEAL HOUSE. Pompeii offers us an exceptionally rich chapter in the history of man because of what it tells us about the houses of ancient times. The city has a great many examples of the "domus", the one-family house as it was between the 4th century B.C. and the lst century A.D.

The basic model was established by the Samnites and was obviously the product of a long history of previous experience. This was the "domus italica", a house with a series of service areas around a central axis with carefully calculated spaces linked to each other. Thus the areas necessary for mainly physical needs, such as the bedrooms, sanitary services, kitchen facilities, dining rooms and so on, lay alongside another series of areas used for the family's social and cultural life. The latter areas were almost completely covered ("atrium" or central hall) or almost completely open-air ("peristylium", or garden patio), while between the atrium and peristyle was the family's most sacred room, the "tablinum". Light and air for all the rooms around them came from the two large central spaces alone, very rarely from the exterior.

This model was so successful that the Romans did not change it for hundreds of years. Their variations to the domus were limited to adding sumptuous decorations and other facilities. The atrium was often embellished with four columns (tetrastyle or Corinthian atrium) and the open-air garden with fountains, statues and nymphaeums. Also added to houses were scenic or rest areas ("exedrae", "diaetae"),

quarters for women ("gynaeceum") or servants, and complete private baths, the "balneum", resembling the public "thermae". Additional floors were also built containing bedrooms and other facilities.

TECHNIQUES AND ART. The **architectural styles** used for buildings were the classical ones, identified by their typical capitals: **Doric** (a plain round capital without decoration), **Ionic** (embellished with large volutes), **Corinthian** (embellished with acanthus leaves) and **Composite** (a combination of Ionic and Corinthian). In the buildings of Pompeii the orders have some characteristics of their own, rooted in particular in the Samnite tradition.

The **types of construction** can also be clearly divided according to the various eras in Pompeii, so that the date each building was begun and the extensions and reconstructions carried out can be established. The first Samnite era (4th-3rd century B.C.) and second Samnite era (200-80 B.C.) saw development from the "opus quadratum" and "opus incertum" techniques to building with blocks of tuff. In the first Roman period (80 B.C. - 14 A.D.) buildings were constructed from irregular pieces of stone and small square blocks forming a diagonal framework. In the second and last Roman period (14-79 A.D.) the use of brick began.

Pompeian wall painting and decoration represents the most interesting aspect of the art of Pompeii, and four distinct styles have been distinguished in these paintings. The **First (Incrustation or Structural) Style** (150-80 B.C.) was so called because its panels and stuccos imitate the coloured marble facing (see House of Sallust, House of the Faun). The **Second (Architectural) Style** (80 B.C. - 14 A.D.) has large paintings with figured compositions alternating with realistic mock architecture (see House of Obelius Firmus, House of the Labyrinth, House of the Silver Wedding, Villa of the Mysteries). The **Third (Egyptianizing or Ornamental) Style** (beginning about 14 A.D.) is predominated by a decorative taste, the painters taking great care over details and doing work with unusually refined technique and colour (see House of M. Lucretius Fronto, House of L. Caecilius Jucundus). In the **Fourth (Illusionist) Style** (beginning about 62 A.D.) the subjects, architecture and perspectives became completely fantastic and overburdened with decorative elements (see House of the Vettii, House of the Lovers, House of Menander, House of Loreius Tiburtinus). Visiting Pompeii - wandering through its streets and squares, seeing the objects left everywhere in the city, but in particular seeing its "domus", the houses brought to light almost intact - is a moving experience because behind the appearance of the houses, so different from our own, we can sense the very human aspirations of a people who, two thousand years ago, accomplished what we still seek today.

PLAN OF A TYPICAL "DOMUS POMPEIANA"

T.O.) "TABERNAE" and "OFFICINAE" - shops and workshops on the outside of a house. The most numerous kinds are : "CAUPONA" - tavern or inn; "THERMOPOLIUM" - selling hot beverages (forerunner to our café); "PISTRINUM" - mill and bakery; "FULLONICA" - laundry, with pressing and dyeing. 1) "ATRIENSIS" - House caretaker and doorkeeper ("Vestibulum" and "Fauces"). 2) "IMPLUVIUM" - pool in the centre of the atrium for catching rain water. On the edge of the pool the sacred table with urn beside it ("Cartibulum" with "Situla"). 3) "COMPLUVIUM" - opening in the roof for letting in light and rain for the "impluvium". 4) Upper floor reached by stairs next to the atrium. 5) "CUBICULA" - bedrooms. 6) "ALA" - living-room areas to the sides of the atrium. 7) "TRICLINIUM" - dining-room with three special couches around the table (brickwork or pieces of furniture). 8) "ANDRON" - access corridor. 9) "VIRIDARIUM" - garden with statues and fountains and, in some cases, a vegetable garden ("Hortus"). A covered colonnade surrounds it ("Peristylium"). 10) "CULINA" - kitchen, in some cases with "Lararium" for the Lares, the household gods; servants' court; "Apotheca", or pantry, and oven. 11) "BALNEUM" - bathing area with rooms and water at different temperatures ("Frigidarium", "Tepidarium", "Calidarium"). 12) "GYNAECEUM" - female quarters. In many houses these quarters, like the servants' and guests' quarters, had their own entrance and atrium connected to the areas where animals and vehicles were kept. 13) Tricliniums for the different seasons, or "OECI", "EXEDRAE" and other living areas situated mainly around the second and larger peristyle. 14) Second "PERISTYLIUM" with large garden almost always present in bigger houses. More than the first peristyle, this garden was embellished by a canal with jets of water and fish ("Euripus"), by small temples, nymphaeums with fountains and statues of gods, pergolas ("Vitea Tecta") and triclinium for dining in the open. 15) "OECUS" and "DIAETAE", living areas which opened onto the large garden. The house almost always had a second or tradesmen's entrance ("Posticum")

On the following two pages:
view from above of the zone of the large Forum, as it was in the Ist century.

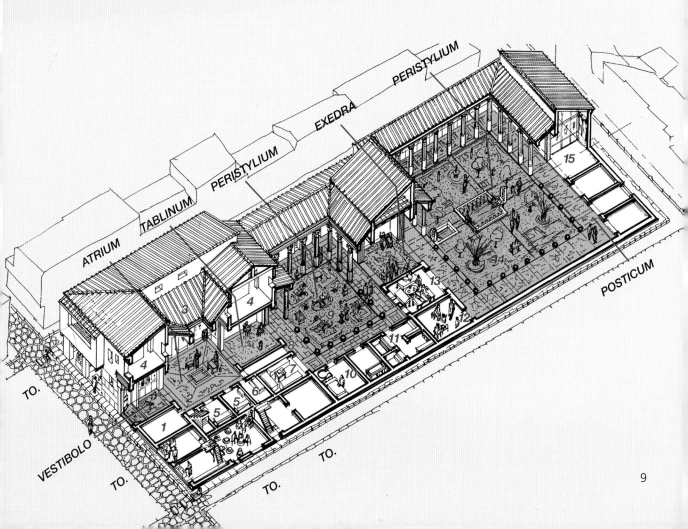

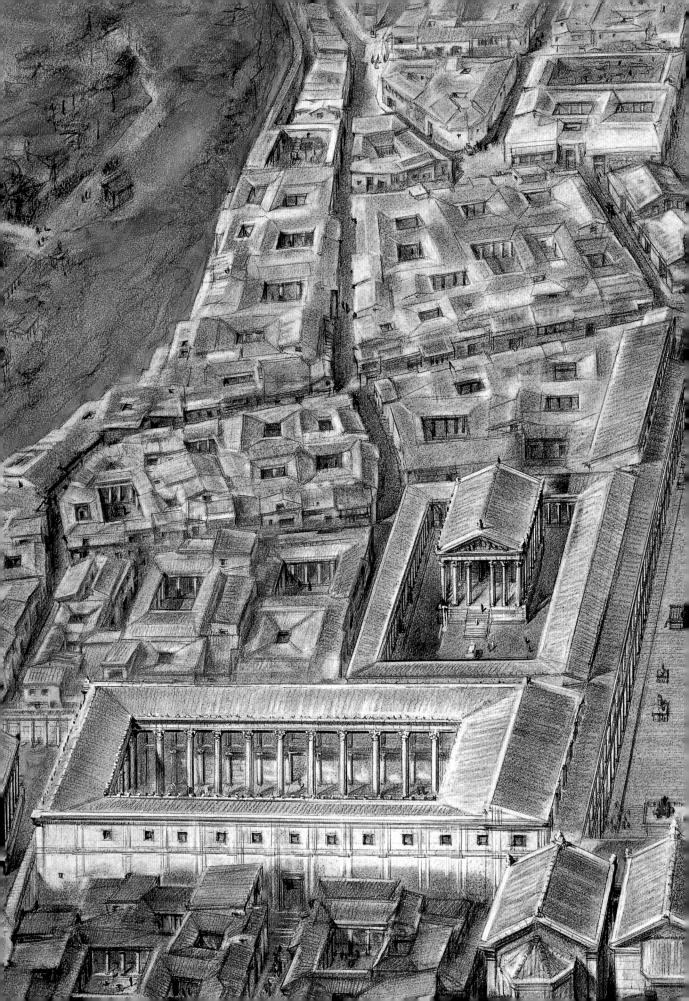

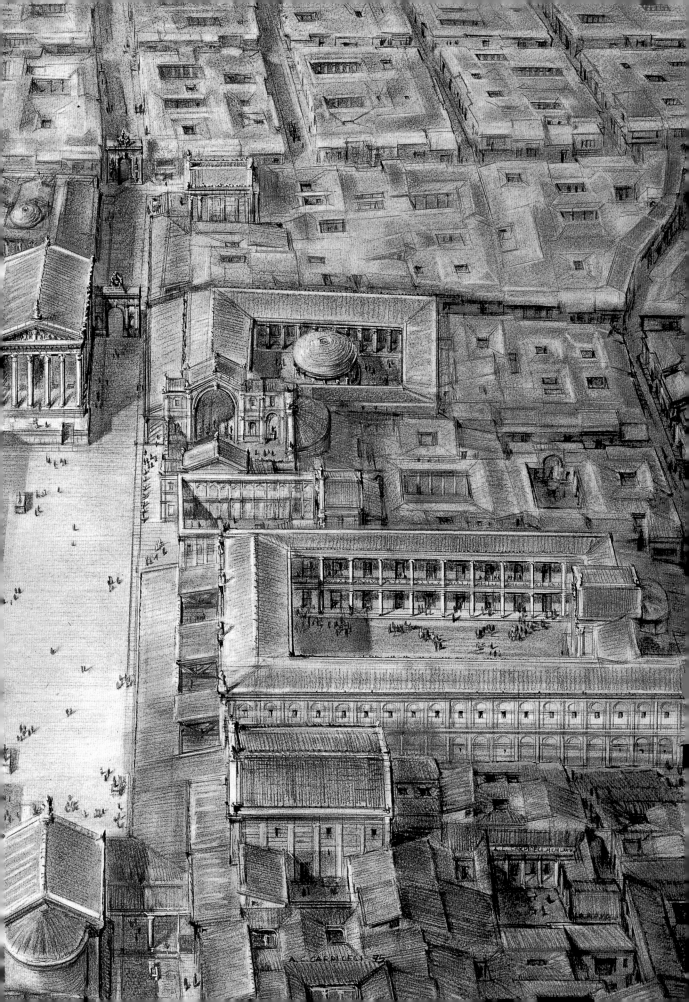

Example of a painting in the First Style:
atrium of the House of Sallust.

Example of a painting in the Third Style:
triclinium of the House of Amandus.

Example of a painting in the Second Style:
Corinthian room in the Villa of the Mysteries.

Example of a painting in the Fourth Style:
triclinium of the House of the Vettii.

Porta Marina.

1 The **PORTA MARINA** is the ancient gate through which one now enters Pompeii. Before passing through it, we should realize that the city once dominated the whole plain as far as the sea, which two thousand years ago was not far away. On the right of the gate are the massive ramparts erected for the temple of Venus which was to be built, on the left the luxurious houses of the « insula occidentalis », the city's western block, and below this the necropolis and the hill which once stretched much further down than it does today. A steep paved ramp leads to the gate's two archways: the left-hand arch was for pedestrians and the right-hand one for animals and light carts carrying salt and fish from the sea. Abutting onto the gate are the remains of what were probably warehouses. In the lower part of the gate can be seen the square blocks belonging to the old Samnite walls, dating from the 4th-2nd century B.C. Inside, the two roads, for carts and pedestrians, continue upwards, still clearly separated, under the one large vault (on the right today is the entrance to the Antiquarium).

Antiquarium: casts of the victims of the eruption.

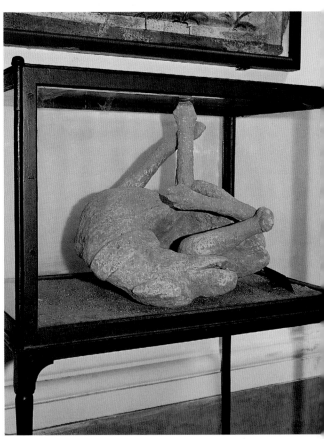

Antiquarium: the altar and the pediment of the Dionysian temple; below: metal fibulas and brooches for clothing.

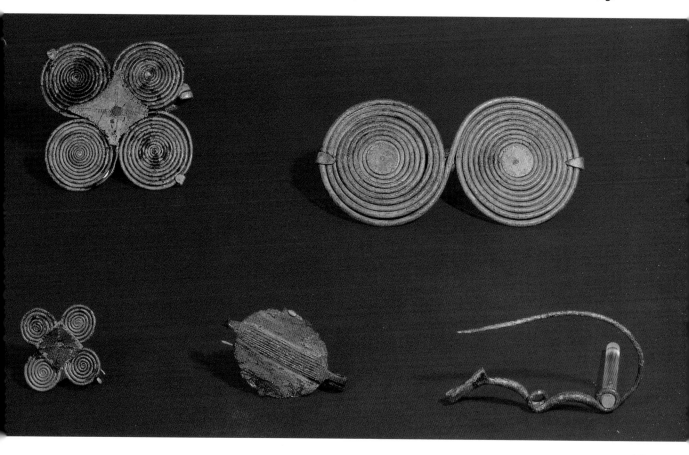

Above: the luxurious houses of the "insula occidentalis"; below: entrance to the House of Romulus and Remus; right: entrance and portico of the Suburban Villa of Porta Marina.

2 The **SUBURBAN VILLA OF PORTA MARINA** is an opulent residence from the Roman era, built alongside the city walls on the right of the Porta Marina tower. The earthquake in 62 A.D. had half-destroyed the villa and the volcanic eruption hit it as it was being rebuilt.

From the long colonnade (80 metres, or nearly 90 yards, long and with 43 columns) there is still a magnificent panoramic view of the sea and mountains. All along the colonnade runs a huge garden. Behind it are the service and living areas, with Pompeii's largest dining room, or triclinium (6 × 8.8 metres, or nearly 20 × 30 feet); its walls are richly decorated in Pompeii's Third Style with extremely interesting panels painted separately and then set in the wall (« pinakes »).

3 The **Temple of Venus** is immediately on the right after passing through the gate. Venus was the patron goddess of Pompeii which, after the Roman conquest, was called « Venus Felix ». The Republican temple was destroyed by the earthquake and the Pompeians must have wanted to ensure that their goddess was protected by building an even bigger temple than the previous one, but the grandiose reconstruction project was halted forever by the eruption of Vesuvius.

Continuing along the Via Marina, on the left are the buildings called the **House of Romulus and Remus** and the **House of Triptolemus**; and finally, after the Temple of Apollo, on the left, and the Basilica, on the right, we enter the great Forum.

Bird's eye view of the forum area showing the main monuments. An idea of what the individual monuments looked like two thousand years ago is provided by comparing this photo with the reconstruction on pages 10-11. On pages 18 and 19: view of the Forum.

A) "AEDILES". Administrative offices. B) "BASILICA". C) "CURIA". Municipal council. D) "DUUMVIRS". City government. E) BUILDING OF EUMACHIA. Fabric market. M) "MACELLUM". Food market. T) BATHS. TA) TEMPLE OF APOLLO. TC) TEMPLE OF AUGUSTUS. TG) TEMPLE OF JUPITER. TL) SHRINE OF THE LARES. TV) TEMPLE OF VESPASIAN.
1) Tribunal in the Basilica. 2) Entrance portico from the Forum to the Basilica. 3) Portico of the Samnite Forum 4, 5, 6, 7) Statues of the Imperial family: Claudius, Augustus, Agrippina, Nero. 8) COMITIUM. Election building. 9) Portico of the Roman Forum. 10) Podiums for auctions. 11) Apse of Building of Eumachia, with its statue of "Concordia Augustea". 12) Statue of the Priestess Eumachia. 13) Ramp to the upper level. 14) House of the Boar. 15) Sacrificial altar in the Temple of Vespasian. 16) Money changers' shops and the monumental entrance to the "Macellum". 17) Tub with dome on twelve columns. 18) Statues of the Imperial family. 19) Fish market. 20) Cella sacred to the Capitoline Triad: Jupiter, Juno and Minerva. 21) Arch of Caligula. 22) Arch of Tiberius. 23) Arch of Germanicus. 24) Forum latrines. 25) "FORUM OLITORIUM". Grain market (now a warehouse for storing archeological materials). 26) "Mensa ponderaria". 27) "Suggestum". Tribune for speakers. 28) Portico of the Roman Forum with two superimposed orders of columns (Doric, Ionic). 29) Apollo shooting an arrow. 30) Herm of Mercury. 31) Altar from the Republican age. 32) Ionic column for sun-dial. 33) Diana shooting an arrow.

The Forum; below: the public buildings.

4 The **FORUM** was the centre of the political, economic and religious life of Pompeii, and access to it was thus restricted to pedestrians. Because of its considerable size (38 × 157 metres, or 125 × 514 feet) and the great public buildings with their own minor squares surrounding it, the Forum could contain all the inhabitants of the city. The colonnade with solid Doric columns made from tuff which can still be seen on the south side was built around the Forum square in the Samnite era. The Romans paved the square with travertine and had begun renovating the colonnade along the long sides, erecting Doric columns, also travertine, with a second order of Ionic columns above. On the south side of the Forum were all the buildings involved in Pompeii's public life: the Basilica, the Municipal Offices and the Comitium. To the right of the Forum, large buildings connected with the city's economy and commerce had been erected, besides religious buildings. Each building was embellished with marble facing and statues, and had its own colonnade facing onto the Forum.

Above: the Basilica with the "Tribunal" in the background; below: the Basilica from the "Tribunal" colonnade.

5 The **BASILICA** (measuring 24 × 55 metres, or 79 × 180 feet) is the oldest and most important public building in the city: built between 120 and 78 B.C., it is the best example in Pompeii of pre-Roman architecture. In the beginning it was also a covered market, but in the lst century A.D. it became the seat of the law courts (handing down civil and commercial judgments). It was then that the « tribunal » was built, an elegant two-level structure on the wall inside the building in the Hellenistic style, with wooden staircases on the sides leading to the upper level. In front of the tribunal is what may have been the base of an equestrian statue of the Emperor Augustus. The side walls were divided into two orders and decorated with imitation marble panels (First Style). Innumerable phrases were scratched on these walls two thousand years ago; in fact one even remarks, « I am astounded, o wall, that you do not crumble under the weight of all these writers ». The main entrance to the Basilica was from the Forum and included a double portico with no less than five doorways. Of the building's three naves the central

one was probably open to the sky. It is interesting to imagine how it must have looked, surrounded by a huge peristyle of 28 fluted Corinthian columns, each one 1.1 metres (3ft 7in) in diameter and about 10 metres (32 ft) high, giving it the appearance of a splendid courtyard.

6 The **Municipal Offices** come immediately after the Basilica on the south side of the Forum. They consist of three large halls, very similar to each other, with niches and apses at the end, once adorned with marbles and statues. In the centre is the **Curia**, seat of the Municipal Council (« Ordo Decurionum »); on the right the hall occupied by the two **Aediles**, who saw to maintenance works in the city; and on the left the hall occupied by the **Duumvirs**, the governors of Pompeii.

The portico facing the Building of Eumachia.

7 The **Comitium**, opposite the Basilica, was the building where elections took place. In its large hall electors, who were divided into « curiae », voted for the lists of candidates before the Duumvir, who was in turn nominated by the elected assembly.

8 The **BUILDING OF EUMACHIA** stands at the beginning of Via dell'Abbondanza. Built by the priestess Eumachia for the corporation of weavers, dyers and launderers (« fullones »), who represented Pompeii's largest industry, the building is as large as the Basilica, consisting of a great courtyard surrounded by a two-storey colonnade. Behind the colonnades were areas used for storing and displaying the cloth after manufacture. Buying and selling took place under the porticos and in the open courtyard. At the end of the portico can still be seen the three great apses: the largest contained the

statue of Livia, wife of the emperor, venerated as Concordia Augustea, and on either side were statues of Tiberius and his brother Drusus. In the gallery behind the large apse the « fullones » had erected a statue of Eumachia, their powerful and generous patroness.

Of the splendid facade facing towards the Forum, only the superb doorway remains, with acanthus leaves all around it, a fine example of the sculptor's art, giving an idea of the extraordinary artistic riches which this building originally had. At the sides of the doorway are two raised niches which were probably used for auction sales. To the right of the facade, at the beginning of Via dell'Abbondanza, can be seen the steps which blocked wheeled vehicles from entering the Forum. Along the street is the long side of the Building of Eumachia, its architectural decorations a series of stucco pilaster strips and arches. On the end corner is the entrance to the large ramp which led to the upper floor of the building.

Above: Temple of Vespasian;
below: marble altar for sacrifices.

9 The **House of the Wild Boar**, on the opposite side of the road at no. 8, is worth visiting because of its fine mosaic pavements in the entrance (the wild boar being attacked by two dogs), in the atrium and in the tablinum (heads in medallions).

10 The **Temple of Vespasian** in the Forum is a much smaller structure than the Building of Eumachia, but not without interest. The sacred area is surrounded by a wall which is decorated with stuccos. Before the small cella (dedicated after the earthquake in 62 A.D. to the worship of the Genius of Vespasian) is the altar, adorned with works of sculpture; on the front of it is an interesting scene depicting the sacrifice of a bull before the temple.

11 The **Temple of the Lares** was begun and completed in the period immediately after the earthquake in 62 A.D. It is a unique building, measuring 18 by 21 metres (59 by 69 feet) and consisting of three large architectural « wings », creating a court in the centre. Both the side wings with their large rectangular niches and the end wing with its great circular niche were covered with marbles and paintings and contained the statues of the tutelary gods of the city (« Lares publici »). The temple was thus a sanctuary which the Pompeians consecrated with solemn ceremonies aimed at expiation and

Above: portico, shops and entrance to the "Macellum"; below: remains of the Temple of the Lares.

propitiation of the gods after the catastrophic earthquake they had lived through.

12 The **MACELLUM** is the last of the series of really big buildings which stood around the Forum. It was a complex built in the Imperial age as a covered market, and had large shops both on the outside, on Via degli Augustali and the Forum, and on the inside, under the colonnade around the large internal square, measuring 37 by 27 metres (121 by 88 ft). In the centre of this square, which still has traces of its rich pictorial decoration on the west wall, was a rotunda with 12 columns covered by a cupola (« tholos ») and containing a fish-pond in the middle. There were three large areas at the end of the square. The central one was dedicated to the Imperial family, and here the statues of Octavia (sister of Augustus) and Marcellus (son of Octavia), now in the National Museum of Naples, were found. Probably the area on the left was a refreshment room and the one on the right was used as a fish market. The facade of the Macellum looking onto the Forum is an interesting one: it contains shops which may have been occupied by the money-changers of the time (« argentarii »). In the centre is the typical double entranceway with an aedicule in the middle, standing on columns, which contained a statue of some member of the Imperial family.

13 On the left of the Temple of Jupiter can be seen the remains of the **Forum Latrines**. Beyond this is a huge storehouse originally used for the sale of grains (« **Forum Olitorium** ») and now turned into a deposit containing a great deal of archeological material. A little further on, in a small recess in the wall of the portico, can be seen the **Mensa Ponderaria**, a travertine table on which are carved the Roman units of measure as a sure check of the measures used in the market.

14 The great **TEMPLE OF JUPITER** stands in isolation dominating the northern side of the Forum. It is a « Capitolium » in pure Italic style, that is, constructed on a high base — measuring 3 metres (10 ft) in height, 37 metres (121 ft) in length and 17 metres (56 ft) in width — with a double flight of steps on the front. The pronaos, or vestibule, is no less than five columns deep, while the cella (which only the priests entered) has a double order of columns around the inside and the typical three niches at the end, occupied by the Capitoline triad: Juno, Jupiter (whose colossal head is in the National Museum of Naples) and Minerva. The temple had underground rooms containing the public treasury (« aerarium ») and the precious objects belonging to the temple itself. Built in 150 B.C., possibly on the site of a previous Etruscan temple, this became Pompeii's main temple when the Roman republic took over. It was renovated under Claudius, but was seriously damaged by the earthquake, and when the volcanic eruption hit it was still being rebuilt, the tiny temple of Jupiter Meilichios near the theatres being used in its place. Originally there were two **triumphal arches** at the sides of the temple. The one on the left was probably dedicated to Germanicus, while

Opposite: remains of the "Forum Olitorium".

View of the Temple of Jupiter as it was before the earthquake in 62 B.C.. At the sides the arches of Germanicus and Tiberius and the porticos on two levels as they were being transformed by the Romans. In front of the porticos to the left: statues of Pompeii's most important citizens and the great podium ("Suggestum") from which orators addressed the crowd.

Above and below: the Temple of Jupiter.

*Above: Temple of Apollo and sacred enclosure
as it appears today; left: the Ionic column for the sundial,
in front of the temple.*

the right-hand one was demolished to give a proper view of the third arch built at the end, as a northern entrance to the Forum, and dedicated to Tiberius (the niches facing towards the Forum may have contained the statues of Nero and Drusus). Traces of the marble which adorned the arches, surmounted by equestrian statues of the emperors, can still be seen. This then was the superb backdrop to the north side of the Forum, with the great Temple of Jupiter in the centre and the two triumphal arches at its sides, and a long series of porticos on two levels (the public could use the second floor to watch various displays in the square below).

15 The **TEMPLE OF APOLLO**, though flanking a long section of the Forum's portico, nevertheless functioned quite independently of the Forum. Thus its alignment and main entrance are on the street leading to the Porta Marina, facing the side of

Temple of Apollo. Above: marble altar; below, from left: bronze statue of Apollo and of Diana.

the Basilica. The temple was erected by the Samnites on a site which the Greeks had consecrated to Apollo's worship as early as the 5th century B.C. The considerable remains of the temple make it easy to imagine what it must have looked like two thousand years ago. The portico, part of which we can see, ran all round the sacred area and temple, and on the wall at the end of it scenes from the Iliad were painted. In front of the columns can still be seen the splendid statue of Apollo on the right and, on the opposite side, the bust of the statue of Diana (the original bronzes are in Naples), both gods in the act of shooting arrows as if in a divine duel. On the bases of the entrance portico were statues of Venus and Hermaphroditus.

The temple is of the Italic type, like the Temple of Jupiter, with an imposing flight of steps leading up the high base to the sacrarium, surrounded by 28 Corinthian columns; two still complete columns stand erect on the front. The vast atrium had six columns along the facade (originally divided in the middle) and was four columns deep. The small sacellum was dominated by the great statue of the god. On the pavement can still be read the Oscan in-

Temple of Apollo and sacred enclosure as it appeared two thousand years ago. A typical Italic temple, it is distinguished by a high podium and deep pronaos with a greater distance between front columns in the centre. In front of it is the marble altar and the Ionic column on which was a sun-dial. All around is a portico with statues of gods and basins for sacrificial water.

scription left by the quaestor Campanius who had it laid down with funds from the temple treasury. Near the secondary exit, behind the temple, was the room occupied by the priest who acted as custodian. In front of the steps can be seen the majestic open-air altar erected in the Republican era. On its left is the Ionic column erected by the duumvirs Sepunius and Erennius for the sun dial. During Nero's rule the whole appearance of the temple was altered by the addition of dense stucco decorations, but these have almost entirely disappeared.

16 The **Temple of Fortuna Augusta** stands at the end of Via del Foro, at the entrance to northern Pompeii, in the area which was the most important urban centre. The building was completely financed by Marcus Tullius, a duumvir re-elected no less than three times, being consecrated in 3 A.D. to the worship of the emperor; along with the Temple of Vespasian, also dedicated to the Imperial family, it was run by the body of priests called the Augustales. It should be noted that these two temples were not grandiose buildings like those most involved in Pompeii's social and religious life, such as the temples in the Forum or, even more so, the Basilica, the Market and the Building of Eumachia.

On the lower part of the temple steps was the open-air altar; access to the upper flight of steps was

*The Temple of Fortuna Augusta as it was
at the beginning of the 1st century B.C.. On the right
is the end of the eastern portico in the Forum,
on the left the intersection of Via di Mercurio
and Via di Nola with the arch surmounted
by the statue of Caligola.*

blocked by a gate. Standing gracefully on its base was the temple facade with its four slender Corinthian columns. A shallow pronaos stood before the cella, inside which part of the central aedicule and the four lateral niches can still be seen. The whole sacrarium was covered with marble facing. One of the statues in the niches was the Emperor Augustus, venerated as « father of the nation ».

On the right of the temple are the shops and portico, a continuation of the Forum porticos; a characteristic of the pillars in the portico is that they have half-columns in front of them. On the left is the beginning of Via degli Augustali, full of shops and houses which were once two-storey. Finally there is an arch over the crossroads, very likely built to support a statue of the emperor Caligula, of which numerous fragments have been found. All the houses, porticos and shops were plastered, many being painted in bright colours and covered with writing, and the crowds of busy people here can easily be imagined.

17 The **Arch of Caligula** stands at the beginning of the picturesque street called **Via di Mercurio**, which leads to the massive Samnite tower and to a view of the ever-present Vesuvius. At the bottom of the arch can still be seen the remains of its travertine facing stone. The deep slits visible at the sides very probably contained supports for shelves on which stood statues or trophies exalting the divinity of the mad and cruel G. Caesar Germanicus, called Caligula, emperor from 37 to 41 A.D. Via di Mercurio was a mainly residential street, full of interesting dwellings as we shall see further on. The buildings had few doors and windows on the ground floor (the shops were almost all at the crossroads) and the first floors were mostly similar to those in Via dell'Abbondanza, that is, they had various openings including windows and loggias and parts jutting out over the street, either balconies or projecting rooms.

On the following page: Via di Mercurio
and the Tower of Mercury seen from the Arch
of Caligula as they appeared nineteen centuries ago.

Above: Via di Mercurio and the Tower of Mercury
seen from the Arch of Caligula; below: two views
of Via di Mercurio.

18 The main entrance to the **FORUM BATHS** is on the street to which the baths give its name, Via delle Terme. These baths, intended mainly for those who came to the Forum from outside the city, were the smallest but most elegant public baths in Pompeii. Built in the early period of the Roman colony by the duumvir Lucius Caesius from public funds, they have the typical features of Roman baths, all the areas needed for the complete bathing cycle (dressing room, cold-water bath, warm-water bath and hot-water bath) and separate sections for men and women. Each room was thoroughly heated with hot air which came from a central furnace and circulated under the floor (« hypocaustum ») or even,

where necessary, in double walls (« concameratio »). An impressive area is the « frigidarium » the form of which recalls the inside of a Renaissance baptistery or chapel. Fine works are the stuccos on the vaults and the series of terracotta « Atlantes » in the « tepidarium ». Also worth seeing are the big bronze brazier in the « tepidarium », which heated it before the central-heating plant came into operation, the great basin for washing face and hands with hot water (it cost 5250 sesterces when placed here), and, on the opposite side, the marble bath tub. These baths are the last of the series of public buildings which stretch uninterrupted from the Porta Marina to the Arch of Caligula.

LAYOUT OF THE FORUM BATHS

MEN'S BATHS - A) Entrance. B) Palaestra entrance. C) Secondary entrance. 1) "APODYTERIUM " - dressing-room. 2) " FRIGIDARIUM " - cold bath. 3) " TEPIDARIUM " - warm bath. 4) " CALIDARIUM "- hot bath. 5) " PALAESTRA ". 6) Bronze brazier and seats. 7) Basin for ablutions. 8) Bath-tub.
FACILITIES - E) Entrance. 9) Furnaces for air and water at different temperatures.
WOMEN'S BATHS. D) Entrance. 10) Dressing-room. 11) Tub for cold bath. 12) " TEPIDARIUM ". 13) " CALIDARIUM ". 14) Open-air courtyard and stairs to the top floor.

Forum Baths. Above: the "Tepidarium"; below: the "Calidarium" (left) and the "Frigidarium".

19 The HOUSE OF THE TRAGIC POET

The **HOUSE OF THE TRAGIC POET** (Ins. VIII, no. 5) is the first interesting residential building in front of the Forum Baths. A typical example of the sort of house acquired and renovated by the class which came to dominate Pompeii economically in its last years, it was adorned with works of art taken, after the first excavations in the 18th century, to the National Museum of Naples. They included paintings in the atrium and peristyle (Sacrifice of Iphigenia, Rape of Briseis, Hera and Zeus) and the mosaic in the tablinum, depicting the rehearsal of a theatrical tragedy, from which the house took its name.

It is easy to imagine how the house must have looked so many centuries ago, with a roof over the atrium and the sun coming in through the compluvium, with the paintings and mosaics, the green of the garden and its little temple adding to the overall light and colour.

House of the Tragic Poet. Left: view of the atrium, tablinum and small garden with lararium as they appear today. On the following page: as they appeared two thousand years ago.

PLAN OF THE HOUSE OF THE TRAGIC POET

B) Shops run by the owner of the house and thus communicating with the vestibule. I) Entrance and vestibule with the "cave canem" (beware of the dog) mosaic on the floor. 1) Servants' stairs. 2) Stairs to the upper floor. 3) Impluvium and marble base of the "Cartibulum" (sacred table in the atrium). 4) "Cubicula" (rest rooms). 5) "Alae" to the sides of the atrium. 6) "Oecus" (living-room) and, next to it, the "Andron" (access corridor). 7) "Culina" (kitchen). 8) "Lararium", the shrine which held the household gods. 9) "Posticum" (secondary entrance)

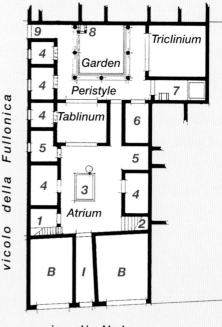

via di Nola

20 The **House of Pansa** (Ins. VI, no. 1) is one of the great upper-class houses which occupied a whole block. It was built by the Samnites and its special feature was a large pool in the peristyle instead of a garden. At the end of the portico, by the kitchen, were the stables and the area occupied by wagons.

21 The **House of M. Fabius Rufus** (Western Ins., no. 19) has been completely excavated only recently. It is one of the largest villa residences, with Fourth Style paintings in the atrium and an interesting little baths complex.

Before Vicolo di Mercurio we encounter what was originally a house but was converted into a **Pistrinum** (Ins. II, no. 3), that is, a bread bakery. The visitor can still see the ancient millstones for grinding the wheat, the old oven with its hood, the grain deposit (« horreum ») and the place where animals were kept (« stabulum »).

22 The **HOUSE OF SALLUST** (Ins. II, no. 4) comes immediately after the street called Vicolo di Mercurio. Though confined between two streets, it exhibits more than any other in Pompeii the nobility and simplicity of proportions of the perfect Samnite house. Around the atrium the remains of decoration in the First or « Structural » Style can still be seen. On the right is a parallel wing, completely transformed in the Roman era, built around a small peristyle with garden (on the right, the winter dining room; on the left, the kitchen; on either side at the end, two bedrooms).

At the sides of the entrance door were no less than six premises converted into shops; the bar in the « thermopolium », on the left, extends inwards as if it were also used by the inhabitants of the great house.

23 The **House of the Surgeon** (Ins. I, no. 9-10) comes after the building occupied by the salt-works corporation (« statio saliniensium »), with plants near the port of Pompeii. This residence, built from blocks of limestone in the 4th-3rd century B.C., derives directly from the ancient Italic type of house. In it many surgical instruments of great historic importance were discovered.

The **House of the Vestals**, next to that of the Surgeon, was a wealthy but fragmented residence, the result of uniting several more modest houses. Almost opposite are the remains of an inn. At the end can be seen the fine gate which led to Herculaneum, the Porta Ercolanense.

House of Pansa: the peristyle.

A section of Via dei Sepolcri.

24 The **PORTA ERCOLANO** (Herculaneum Gate, also called the « Porta Saliniensis ») was entirely rebuilt under the Emperor Augustus, when the walls and gates no longer served any defensive purpose. In fact it resembles an arch of triumph, with the central archway for wheeled traffic and the two minor arches, at the sides, for pedestrians. On the right can be seen the ancient « agger », the rampart which acted as a buttress to the wall and also allowed the defenders to reach the top of the fortifications; on the inside of the rampart the remains of Greek walls from the 5th century B.C. have been found.

Between the Porta Ercolano and the other gate called the Porta Vesuvio (leading to Vesuvius) can be seen the walls and towers built by the Samnites to defend themselves against Roman attacks; near the gates, in the great blocks of tuff, are the deep holes made by the stone projectiles hurled against the walls by Sulla's military machine when he crushed the city in the Social war in 89 B.C.

25 The **VIA DEI SEPOLCRI** (meaning street of tombs) begins immediately after the Porta Ercolano. The tombs have villas and commercial buildings constructed among them. Worth noting on the north side are: the **Villa with the Mosaic Columns** (half uncovered), which has a fine fountain and the remains of 3rd century B.C. tombs in the garden; and the **Portico of the Tabernae**, a series of shops each one of which had a small dwelling attached with a « coenaculum » (dining room) on the upper floor. On the south side is the great complex called the **Villa of Cicero**, excavated and buried again in 1763, where fine paintings and mosaics, now in Naples, were found. Among the tombs which follow, worth noting are: the stuccos showing gladiatorial games in honour of **Umbricius Scaurus** (rich maker of « garum », a famous sauce of Pompeii), and the reliefs showing a funeral ceremony and a ship mooring, sculpted on the **tombstone of C. Munatius** (his wife, Naevoleia Tyche, had the tomb erected).

Top: tomb of Mamia in the form a semi-circular seat
and mausoleum with columns of the Istacidi family.
Bottom: sepulchre with decorated chapel.

Monuments outside
the Porta Ercolano

A) Embankment of the walls with the steps
giving access to the sentry's walk. P)
"Pomerium", sacred road around the walls.
TM) Series of shops with portico on the street.
S) Samnite Necropolis from 3rd century B.C. TG)
Long series of shops with portico along the
street. X) Street which probably led to the fresh
and salt water baths of M. Crassus Frugi. Z)
Zones still unexplored. Y) Modern street which
leads today to the Villa of the Mysteries.

TOMBS. First section. 1) Niche tomb of the
"Augustalis" M. Cerrinius Restitutus. 2) Seat
tomb ("schola") of the duumvir Aulus Veius. 3)
Altar tomb of M. Porcius. 4) Seat tomb of the
priestess Mamia. 5) Small temple-type
mausoleum with ring of columns, of the Istacidi
family. 6) Large altar tomb with base of volcanic
stone and cornice in travertine. 7) Tomb built by
Fabia Sabina for her husband, the aedile M.
Terentius Maior, with a contribution of 2000
sesterces from the Pompeians. 8) Tomb with enclosure. 9) Tomb of the Garlands, so called
because of the elegant decorations between the
pillars. 10) Tomb of the Blue Vase, so called
because of the fine glass vase with cupids har-
vesting grapes, now in Naples. 11) Small funeral
chapel decorated with stuccos (note seashell in
bowl, tritons and dolphins on the front) with
seat on the inside for passers-by.
Second section. 12) Unfinished altar tomb for
Servilia. 13) Tomb erected by the decurions in
honour of the merchant Umbricius Scaurus. 14)
Circular mausoleum. 15) Tomb of the
"Augustalis" Gaius Calventius Quietus. On
the marble altar is a representation of the
"bisellium" (theatre seat equal to that of the
decurions) with which he had been honoured.
16) Tomb in the form of a triclinium of Istacidius
Helenus. 17) Mausoleum with a tombstone over
a funeral chamber built by Naevoleia Tyche for
her husband C. Munatius "pagan", meaning a
resident of the suburb ("pago") of Pompeii,
Augustus Felix. 18) Triclinium-shaped tomb of
Gnaeus Vibrius Saturninus. 19) Chamber tomb
with marble door. 20) Tomb in travertine built by
the priestess Alleia Decimilla for her husband, a
duumvir, and her son, a decurion. 21) Tomb of
the Ceia "gens" (family). 22) Tomb with
rustication and pilaster strips of the Arris
"gens".

VILLA OF DIOMEDES a) Entrance. b) Peristyle.
c) Small peristyle. d) Bath areas. d) Room with
apse and antechamber. f) Tablinum. g) Triclinium. h) Covered terrace. i) Open-air terrace. l)
Pavillon-belvedere. m) Large garden with portico
and cryptoporticus. n) Swimming pool and fountain. o) Summer triclinium.

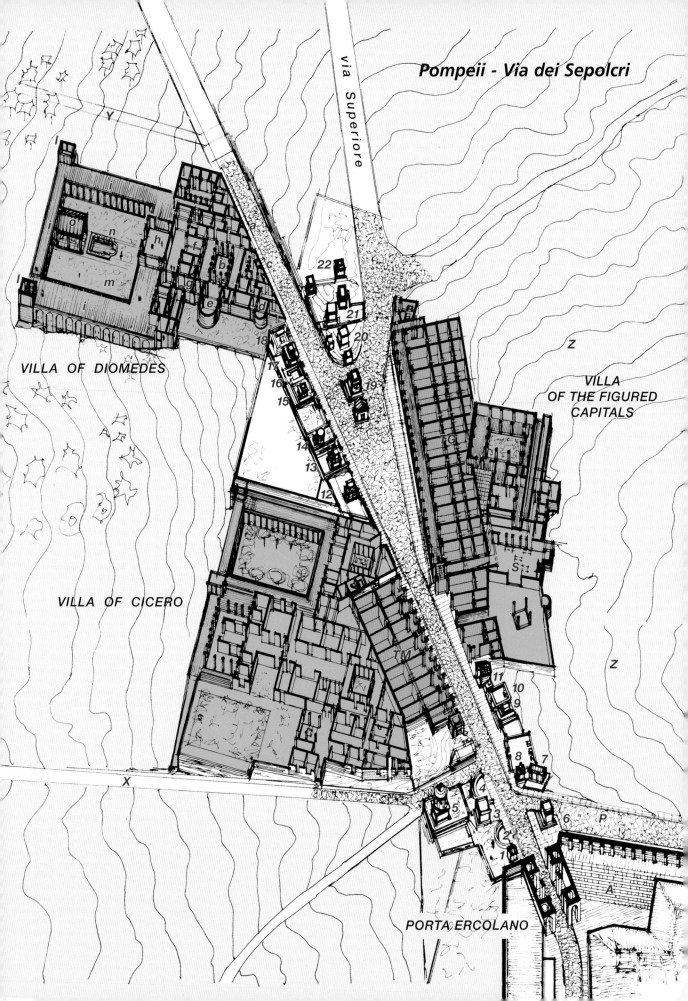

Pompeii - Via dei Sepolcri

Villa of Diomedes: general view and detail of the atrium-peristyle.

26 At the end of the necropolis to the south is the **VILLA OF DIOMEDES**. After the excavations and plundering in the 18th century, very little is left of the villa's ancient grandeur, but its layout still suggests the noble dimensions of what was one of the largest of Pompeii's suburban villas. The complex seems to have been carefully designed both inside and out, to make the most of the splendid views; thus its prospect is towards the west, and it was built on two different levels.

The villa is built around an atrium with peristyle, which are linked to the large garden, on a lower level. Above the porticos which ran all the way round the garden was a « solarium », a sun terrace, and an « ambulatio », for walks in the open air; at the ends were two covered towers from which the view of the sea could be enjoyed. Under the porticos is a large covered gallery, or cryptoporticus, which in the villa's last period was being converted into a cellar to contain amphoras full of wine, apparently to meet the requirements of its last owner, who must have been an important wine merchant.

Villa of Diomedes as it was two thousand years ago.
Note the dominant upper levels of the villa
and the large garden of the lower level,
protected from wing by the portico surrounding it.
In the garden: the monumental swimming pool
and triclinium for open-air dining. To the left
of the vilLla: the farm area.

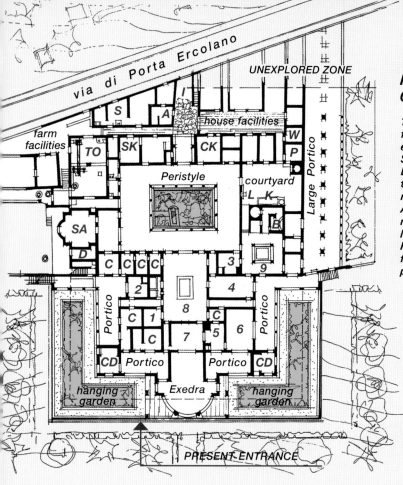

via di Porta Ercolano

UNEXPLORED ZONE

farm facilities

house facilities

PLAN OF THE VILLA OF THE MYSTERIES

1) Carriage entrance (not yet accessible). A) Offices. S) Farm facilities. SK) Farm and kitchen equipment. TO) Wine press and equipment. CK) Servants' kitchen. K) Kitchen. L) Lararium. P) Bakery. B) Bathing areas. C) Bedrooms. D) Pantries and storerooms. CD) Rooms for daytime rest.
ARCHITECTURAL PAINTINGS. 1) Simple colonnade. 2) Peristyle with arches. 3) Peristyle with lintels. 4) Colonnade with festoons.
FIGURE PAINTINGS. 5) Dancing satyr and other figures. 6) Dionysiac mysteries. 7) Egyptian-style paintings. 8) Tuscan atrium. 9) Tetrastyle atrium.

Peristyle

courtyard

Large Portico

Portico

Portico

Portico

Portico

hanging garden

Exedra

hanging garden

27 The **VILLA OF THE MYSTERIES**, because of its paintings, is one of the most important classical villas to have been discovered. In the 2nd century B.C. the villa was a simpler structure, but in later periods it was repeatedly enlarged and rebuilt, new floors being added. After the earthquake in 62 A.D., the new owners were converting it into a farm. Entry to the villa at present is via the rooms on the side facing the sea, but the entrance was on the opposite side and was so large that even carts could pass through it.

All the decorations on the ground floor are in the Second Style (except for those in the tablinum, which are in the Third Style and include fine miniatures on a black background revealing Egyptian taste). One series of these decorations is the marvellous **architectural paintings**: those in the room near the small atrium are still rough in technique, but they are more refined in the room to the left of the tablinum, and are superb in the room with double alcove, not far away (note the porticos with arches, the entrance door, the cornices with corbels and the central arch with view of a circular temple). Finally, in the « oecus », the room to the south of the atrium, there are yet more magnificent colonnades with festoons and an entrance door. The other series of

decorations consists of the outstanding **figured paintings**, making up a cycle, in two adjacent rooms. On the walls of the first are seven panels containing isolated but superbly painted figures. And in the second, larger room is an unforgettable sight: as we look all round the room, we are watching a Dionysiac rite, performed for us by 29 actors, a wordless and solemn rite, full of profound mystery, which slowly unfolds so that the figures, symbols and objects seem to take on a life of their own existing outside the world of reality.

The frieze, 3 metres high and 17 metres long (10 ft by 56 ft), depicts the initiation of a woman into the Dionysiac mysteries - a cult widespread in Campania and Etruria, and with many followers throughout Italy, despite the severe sanctions decreed against it by the Roman Senate. It is thought that these fine paintings, along with those of the antechamber, were painted by an artist from Campania in the 1st century B.C., commissioned by the woman who owned the villa, a priestess and initiate of the cult of Dionysus, portrayed in the figure of the matron to the right of the entrance. In addition, all the painted figures are depicted with features that make it probable that they are portraits of people who actually existed, living on as eternal symbols.

*Overlooking the sea, the facade of Villa of Mysteries
as it was about two thousand years ago.
Note the rotunda with its windows looking towards
the sea and with two small hanging gardens
at its sides.*

Villa of the Mysteries. Above: view of the exterior; below: peristyle.

Villa of the Mysteries: details of some wall paintings in the interior.

1   2   3   4   5   6   7   8

12   13   14   15   16   17   18   19

9 10 11

DESCRIPTION OF THE DIONYSIAC RITES

" CATECHESIS ". Young Dionysus (2) reads the ritual to the initiate (1). The woman initiator (3) watches and holds a " volumen " in her left hand. - " AGAPE SACRA ". The young woman making the offering (4) approaches the priestess in charge of the ceremony (6) who is assisted by attendants (5,7). - Pastoral scene with Silenus (8) playing a lyre in ecstasy at the divine vision. A young female " Pan " (9) plays a pan-pipe and a female satyr (10) suckles a fawn. - The terrified initiate (11) is about to retreat after seeing the flagellation scene on the opposite wall. - Group with Silenus (12) giving a drink to a young satyr (13) while another young satyr (14) holds up a frightening mask. - Marriage of the god Dionysus (15) and Ariadne (16), symbolizing the divine happiness awaiting the initiates. - A standing initiate (17) and another on her knees (18) about to uncover the " mistica vannus " or " phallos ", symbol of fertility. - Implacable divinity with black wings (19) raises the " flagellum " to strike the initiate (20), who desperately tries to hide her head in the lap of her companion (21). - The last trial has been overcome and the newly initiated woman (22) dances ecstatically. Before her is the assistant (23) with the long " thyrsos " (sacred staff). - Toilet of the newly initiated woman (26) as she prepares for her divine marriage; her companion (25) continues to help her while a cupid (24) holds a mirror and another (27) admires her beauty.

20   21   23 22   24   25   26   27

Via di Mercurio seen from the Tower of Mercury.

28 The **Tower of Via Mercurio**, reached by coming back along Via Consolare and going to the end of Via di Mercurio, is the eleventh tower in the walls of Pompeii and was built by the Samnites a short time before the siege by the Romans under Sulla. By standing on the roof terrace of the tower we can admire the stupendous **Panorama of Pompeii**, crowned by Vesuvius, the Lattari peaks and the sea.

29 The **House of Apollo** (Ins. VII, no. 23) is immediately to the right going back along Via di Mercurio. The facade still retains its original severe appearance. The inside of the house was completely redone with Fourth Style decorations, and traces of these can be seen in the imitation colonnade with its painted niches at the end of the garden, in the theatrical architecture depicting scenes of « Apollo and Marsyas » in the room with two beds, and lastly in the landscapes and the mosaic depicting Achilles being recognized on Scyros outside the cubiculum. Also worth noting is the graceful fountain at the end to the right of the tablinum.

30 The **House of Meleager** (Ins. IX, no. 2) comes next on the left of this street. It is a noteworthy Samnite building decorated in the last Roman period. Mercury and Fortune are seen at the entrance; in the atrium is a marble table at the base of which can still be seen a container for keeping food fresh under water. Due to the limited space, the peristyle with its garden was built to the left of the atrium. At the centre of the peristyle is a large reception room with an internal colonnade (« hoecus corinthius »).

31 The **House of the Centaur** (Ins. IX, no. 5) is next, again on the left. This is another example of three houses converted into one. It is worth noticing the room to the right of the entrance, decorated in the First Style (« Structural »).

32 The **House of Adonis** (Ins. VII, no. 58), on the opposite side of the street, is famous for the large painting which takes up almost an entire wall of the garden and depicts the scene « Adonis with Venus and Cupids ». The small paintings of the « Toilet of Hermaphroditus » in a room to the left are also interesting.

33 The **House of Castor and Pollux** (Ins. IX, nos. 6-7) is yet another dwelling obtained from the union of three earlier houses. The Corinthian-type atrium is the richest in columns which surround the impluvium. Note the small paintings in the rooms at the end: « Birth of Adonis », « Scylla and Minos », « Apollo and Daphne », « Nymph, Silenus and young Bacchus ».

Tower of Mercury.

House of Castor and Pollux.

House of Meleager: peristyle.

Fountain in the House of the Large Fountain.

The garden in the House of the Anchor as it appears today.

34 The **Caupona of Via di Mercurio** (Ins. X, no 1) is the tavern on the corner of the alley of the same name. It has a sales counter, shelves in steps for crockery and the kitchen. In the back of the shop a series of small paintings can be seen: carts with wine-skins, players, travellers drinking, wearing their typical hooded capes, and the serving boy. They are scenes which bring back to life the taverns of ancient Pompeii.

35 The **House of the Small Fountain** (Ins. VII, nos. 23-24), immediately after the crossroads, takes its name from a mosaic fountain which it contains. On the walls of the nymphaeum, traces of landscapes with villas and country and seaside houses can still be seen.

36 The **HOUSE OF THE LARGE FOUNTAIN** (Ins. VIII, no. 22), next to the preceding house, also has, at the end of the tablinum, an admirable fountain with glass-paste mosaics and stuccos and delightful bronze statues (the originals in Naples). Their liveliness has remained unchanged even after twenty centuries, and in them we can still appreciate the colours and motifs of the wall decorations and fabrics of the time. The doorway made of carefully squared blocks of tuff is also interesting.

37 The **Fullonica** (Ins. VIII, no. 20), beside the House of the Large Fountain, is the largest workshop in Pompeii for washing and dying wool fabric. This vast « fullonica » was built in a former aristocratic residence: the tubs were placed along the portico, and on the left side were the bronze basins used for pressing the cloth, the wash-tub, the press, and finally the deposit area for the washed and ironed fabric ready to be consigned to customers.

38 The **HOUSE OF THE ANCHOR** (Ins. X, no 7) is almost at the end of Via di Mercurio, in the direction of the Arch of Caligula. The name is taken from the mosaic anchor in the entrance, perhaps symbolizing the owner's maritime activity. Small in size with an irregular plan, this house has an extremely interesting garden: it extends along the

The garden in the House of the Anchor as it was about two thousand years ago. Today, little is left of what was once one of the finest gardens in the medium-size homes of Pompeii, originally embellished and sheltered by a second floor with portico surmounting the cryptoporticus running all around.

right side, taking up more than half of the limited area available.

Very little is left of the architectural and decorative wealth that this internal court once had, but it is not difficult to reconstruct it in one's imagination: its paintings, mosaics and stucco decorations, especially in the aedicule and niches at the end; the portico with pillars and columns all around the upper floor; and the greenery, flowers and large and small sculptures throughout the garden (see reconstruction on previous page).

39 The **HOUSE OF THE FAUN** (Ins. XII, nos. 2-5) is on Via della Fortuna beyond the point where it crosses Vico del Fauno (named after the house).

It is the most beatuful example of a « domus » surviving from ancient times; it occupies the entire area bounded by the four roads (a block of almost 40 metres × 110 metres, or 128 ft by 352 ft) and has in particular abundance all those features common to Pompeii's other aristocratic houses.

Very likely, as is generally supposed, it was built for Publius Sulla, nephew of the conqueror of the Samnite city, who had the task of organizing and reconciling the old and new interests of the Roman Republic at Pompeii (the step at the entrance and door which opens to the outside are signs of special distinction). It had two atriums: one for the main part

PLAN OF THE HOUSE OF THE FAUN.

1) "VESTIBULUM" with double door; on the floor the welcome inscription "have". 2) "FAUCES", entrance flanked by two shrines for the Lares, the household gods. 3) Large Tuscan "Atrium" with impluvium in "opus sectile" (small tesserae of coloured marble) and the fountain of the Dancing Faun. 4) "CUBICULA". 5) "ALAE". 6) "TABLINUM". 7) "TRICLINIUM" for winter meals and "TRICLINIUM" for autumn meals. 8) Garden and peristyle with Ionic columns. 9) Entrance to the guests' and servants' quarters. 10) Tetrastyle atrium (with four columns) and guest areas. 11) Stairs for upper floor. 12) Access to servants' area. 13) Stable and coach house. 14) Bathing areas. 15) Kitchen. 16) Pantry. 17) Summer tricliniums. 18) "EXEDRA" which once had the famous mosaic of Alexander now in Naples. 19) Large garden. 20) Large peristyle, at one time with two orders of columns (Doric and Ionic). 21) "POSTICUM" (secondary entrance). 22) Areas for gardener and door-keeper.

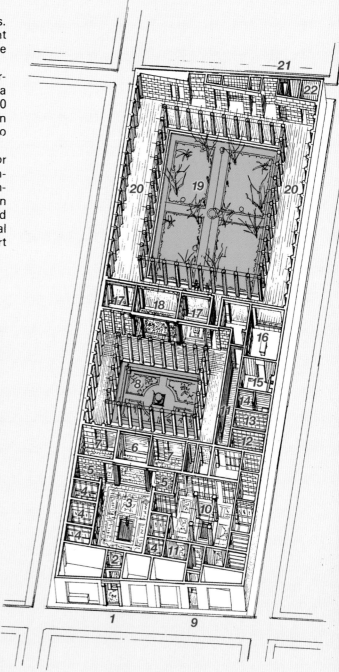

House of the Faun: the present state of one of the most illustrious dwellings in the ancient world.

of the « domus », and the other, to the right, with four colums in the middle (tetrastyle) and with its own entrance for a separate part of the house, perhaps used for guests. It also had two peristyles each with its own garden, the one at the end being exceptionally large, with two orders of columns and a back entrance.

The main atrium is Tuscan in style (without columns), and here one can see the lovely impluvium, with its rich geometrical inlays of coloured marbles and its beautiful small statue of the dancing Faun (the original is in Naples). It is easy to imagine the covering of the atrium with light entering through it and to see, through the tablinum, the original perspective created by the long flight of columns, shimmering in the light and surrounded by the greenery of the gardens: in the middle of it all is the Faun, blithely dancing with his face turned upwards, almost as if to challenge the sun. The marble support of the central fountain (« labrum ») is still to be seen in the smaller peristyle.

The large peristyle was undoubtedly one of the biggest: two orders of columns, completely surrounding the area; that is no less than 88 columns which were some four metres (about 12 ft) high, Doric on the ground floor and perhaps Ionic on the upper level. The outside perimeter measures 38 metres × 44 metres (122 ft × 141 ft) and the inside one is approximately 27 by 30 metres (86 × 96 ft). It is interesting to try to imagine how this portico must have been, reflecting what was being built in the Forum, adorned with a garden, and certainly furnished with art works (« ars topiaria »); and thus we can envision this extremely pleasant court, a worthy ancestor to the Renaissance courts fourteen centuries later.

The small and large peristyles are separated by the « Exedra », the most illustrious room in this great house, not only because of the columns at the sides of the large entrance room (First Style decorations on the walls), but also for the mosaic which once stretched out across the floor like a luxurious carpet (in the centre was the famous mosaic depicting the « Battle between Alexander the Great and Darius, King of the Persians », now in the National Museum of Naples). Other beautiful mosaics, at one time in the triclinium to the left, the atrium wings and the winter triclinium (all at the National Museum of Naples), together with the balanced distribution of spaces and volumes, the sober, First-Style wall decorations, the beautiful peristyles rich in greenery and the architecture contributed to make this one of the most illustrious private dwellings in the ancient world.

The House of the Faun as it appeared nineteen centuries ago. View of the atrium with its impluvium and of the tablinum; at the back can be seen the columns of the two peristyles and the exedra.

The Battle between Alexander the Great and Darius,
King of the Persians, the famous mosaic of the floor
in the "exedra" of the House of the Faun,
now in the National Museum of Naples.

40 The **House of the Black Wall** (Reg. VII, Ins. IV, no. 59) is in front of the House of the Faun. The wall that gives the house its name is found in a room behind the peristyle. The Cupids painted on panels must have made a remarkable effect against the background when it still had all its brilliance. Worth noting too is the elegant peristyle with one side decorated with stucco half-columns.

41 The **House of the Figured Capitals** (Ins. IV, no 57) is yet another example of a Samnite house. The capitals, on which are depicted a bacchant and a married couple, were in the entrance, and can be seen today in the Antiquarium. In the garden are a sun-dial and the Lararium.

A little further on is the secondary entrance to the **House of Ariadne** or **of the Coloured Capitals** (Ins. IV, no 51) which are in the peristyle (Samnite capitals stuccoed and painted by the Romans). The main entrance to this large house is on Via degli Augustali. Worth noting are: the deep pool in the garden and the paintings in the Fourth Style (with figures and landscapes) in the peristyle area.

Following this house is the **House of the Hunt** (no. 48) with its Samnite facade. Inside are traces of rich decoration (the best preserved examples are in Naples), including Autumn and Winter in the atrium, mythological paintings in the bedrooms, and the large scene of the wild animal hunt painted on the back wall of the garden.

42 The **HOUSE OF THE LABYRINTH** (Reg. VI, Ins. XI, nos 9-10) lies at the back of the House of the Faun. This is another large house from the Samnite period, with two atriums of which the main one contains four columns (tetrastyle). Also luxurious are the reception areas and especially the central hall at the end of the peristyle which has an internal colonnade (« hoecus corinthius »), and on the walls, fine architectural paintings in the Second Style, so similar to the decorations in the Villa of the Mysteries that they seem painted by the same artist (also note the small round temple). The mosaic depicting Theseus and the Minotaur in the Labyrinth is inlaid in the floor of the room next to the hall. Note also the large peristyle, for the most part still intact.

House of the Labyrinth. Above: peristyle; below: painted architecture in the "oecus".

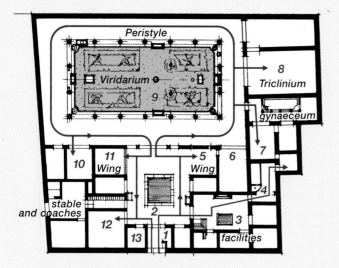

PLAN OF THE HOUSE OF THE VETTII

NOTE: The suggested route for seeing the most interesting works is indicated in red. The numbers referring to the various areas are given in the text along with the descriptions of the works.

Following page: fresco showing Priapus, god of fertility.

43 The **HOUSE OF THE VETTII** (Ins. XV, no 1) has been brought to light almost completely intact thanks to the diligent and precise excavation works done a century ago.

It was a modest-sized dwelling owned by two rich merchants: Aulus Vettius Restitutus and Aulus Vettius Conviva, who spent substantial sums of money not just to have the house decorated, but to show off their wealth. The house was built along two adjoining sides of the peristyle, taking up slightly more than half of the available area. In the area not used for the main rooms are the female quarters and the service areas that undoubtedly continued on the upper level, now destroyed. More than the architecture, one should admire the stupendous pictorial decorations which constitute an incomparable « in situ » picture-gallery showing the Fourth Style of Pompeii, done after the earthquake in 62 A.D.

(Note: this description follows the itinerary with numbers as shown on the map). 1 - VESTIBULE. Covered: Priapus, god of fertility, wards off the evil eye of those envious of the wealth of the owners. 2 - ATRIUM. At the sides two strong-boxes; on the walls fine decorations with friezes of Cupids and Psyche. 3 - SMALL ATRIUM. To the right: Small temple-type Lararium painted with the Genius of the « pater familias » between two Lares (household gods), and below their feet, the large serpent « agathodémone » who drinks from the offerings. 4 - SMALL COURT WITH KITCHEN. A tripod with cauldron can still be seen in the fireplace; at the back toward the women's quarters, room with pornographic figures. 5 - RIGHT WING OF ATRIUM. Medallions with heads of Medusa and Silenus. 6 - OECUS TO RIGHT OF PERISTYLE. Plinth with imitation marbles; large panels on mock architecture with divinities (at top), at the bases small panels with seascapes and masks. On the corner panels, couples of dancing bacchants. In the three large paintings with figures, starting from the wall at left: Daedalus presenting the wooden cow to Pasiphae; Ixion tied to the wheel by Vulcan with the angry Juno present and Nephele at his feet in anguish for her lover Ixion; Dionysus surprising the sleeping Ariadne. 7 - TRICLINIUM IN FEMALE QUARTERS. Paintings of: Ulysses recognizing Achilles; Hercules surprising Augeas. 8 - LARGE TRICLINIUM. Red panels on walls with black decorated pillars (the small panels painted on wood and inlaid in the centre of each wall have been lost). Along the plinth, creating an almost cinematographic effect, are scenes of cupids imitating adult occupations. From right to left: target practice with stones, flower vendors, manufacturers and sellers of perfumes and drugs (note cupboard for health-giving oils, counter with scales and prescription book, and a Psyche being cured by a Cupid), chariot-racers, craftsmen of metals and precious stones, washers and dyers (fullones), festivities of the goddess Vesta (« Vestalia »), grape-gatherers, festivities and triumph of Bacchus. These scenes seem to summarize what most interested the Pompeians. In the small paintings on black background: Psyche picking flowers. Near the central panels on the long walls: to the right, Agamemnon about to kill the deer sacred to Diana and Apollo slaying the python; to the left Orestes and Pylades before King Thoas and Iphigenia. In the panels are famous couples from mythology (from the right): Perseus and Andromeda, Dionysus and Ariadne, Apollo and Daphne, Neptune and Amymone, Hermaphroditus and Silenus. At the top, fanciful architectural features with figures of divinities. 9 - PERISTYLE. Wall decorations with architectural motifs on a light background appearing between the large panels. The flower-beds in the garden have been faithfully reconstructed along the lines left by the original ones, and all the fountains around them are fed through the same lead pipes of nineteen centuries ago. Thus we see the garden full of satyrs and splendid cupids and hear once again the soft music of its fountains from

the distant past. 10 - OECUS TO LEFT OF PERISTYLE. Paintings placed in large architectural aedicules. At the sides three windows containing mock architectural features. In the paintings, starting from left: Hercules as a child strangling the serpents sent by Juno, Pentheus slain by the Bacchants, Dirce imploring Amphyon and Zeus as they tie her to the enraged bull. 11 - WING TO LEFT OF ATRIUM. Scenes of fighting cocks. 12 - OECUS OF ATRIUM. Small paintings depicting: Cyparissus grieving after killing the deer sacred to Apollo, Pan fighting with Cupid. At the top, mock architecture with Leda, Danae and Jupiter enthroned. 13 - CELLA. Beneath the frieze small paintings done by another and less important artist: Ariadne abandoned, Hero and Leander. In the frieze: fish-pond.

House of the Vettii. Right: lararium; below: view of the peristyle and garden.

*House of the Vettii. Frescoes in the oecus of the atrium, illustrating the myth of Cyparissus,
the young hunter who slew the stag dear to Apollo.*

House of the Vettii. Above: one of the decorations in the atrium; below: detail of the frieze in the triclinium.

House of the Vettii. Above: view of the paintings in the "oecus";
below: Hercules as a child strangling the serpents (left) and detail of Ixion tied to the wheel by Vulcan.

44 The **HOUSE OF THE GILDED CUPIDS** (Ins. XVI, no 7). This is another wealthy home, to the right of the House of the Vettii. It belonged to Poppaeus Abitus (perhaps a relative of Poppaea, wife of Nero), and again shows the refined taste of Pompeii's new wealthy classes. Besides the rich decorations and pavements, one should note the skill with which this newer dwelling was constructed over an older one: it utilizes the limited space available, despite the irregular site, and is distributed around the peristyle and garden.

Much of the original elegance has come down to us thanks to the ability of the archeologists working at the beginning of this century. There are many mosaic and painted works to see. In two « cubicula » to the sides of the atrium: Paris, Mercury, Leda and the swan, Narcissus at the spring. At the back of the tablinum: Paris and Helen at Sparta. In the triclinium which links the atrium to the peristyle, paintings in the Third Style including: Thetis in the workshop of Vulcan, Jason and Pelias, Achilles, Briseis and Patroclus. The peristyle is especially interesting; the colonnaded doorway is elevated as if it were meant

*House of the Gilded Cupids. Above: Thetis
in the workshop of Vulcan; right: Venus as Fisherwoman;
preceding page, top: peristyle and garden;
bottom: marble relief.*

to be an open-air stage (« pulpitum »). Between its
columns are marble discs (« oscilla ») and masks.
The garden is full of busts on small pillars (herms)
and excellent bas-relief sculptures around the pool
and fountain. On the north side of the peristyle is a
graceful small lararium-temple, and on the south side
a shrine dedicated to the Egyptian goddess Isis. In
the « oecus » to the right of the triclinium are paintings depicting Diana and Actaeon, Leda and Venus
as Fisherwoman. In the north corner: the kitchen, the
secondary exit, and the rooms decorated on black
background in which part of the ceiling decorations
has also been restored. Next to this: a small room in
which glass discs engraved with cupids painted on
gold leaves have been inserted in the walls.

House of the Silver Wedding: atrium tetrastylus.

45 Continuing north, we find the **House of the Prince of Naples** (Ins. XV, no. 8) which is small but elegant. Worth noting is the graceful Silenus bearing the young Bacchus, sculpted on the marble supports of a mensa and a typical small lararium-temple with arch.

At the end of this alley: the **Porta Vesuvius** and the « **Castellum Aquae** ». The latter is a splendid, simple construction, with a blind arcade made of bricks erected against the massive blocks of the walls. Inside it is a large circular cistern where the water coming from the Augustan aqueduct was filtered through lead diaphragms before being distributed to the city.

46 The **Necropolis of Porta Vesuvius** is immediately outside. To the left, among the cypresses, can be seen the **tomb of Vestorius Priscus**, erected by his mother. The tomb has the form of an altar inside a fence decorated with scenes of the after-life. Returning along Via di Stabia one can see the deep furrows left by the heavy traffic of carts travelling along this « cardo maximus », one of the city's main streets. Further north is a small,

elegantly decorated dwelling, the **House of the Ara Maxima** (Ins. XVI, no. 15). Beyond it, turning left on Via di Mercurio, we reach the House of the Silver Wedding.

47 The **HOUSE OF THE SILVER WEDDING** (Reg. IV, Ins. II, i), on the edge of the area excavated late last century, was a dwelling almost as wealthy as that of the Vettii, but more imposing because of its original Samnite structure, renovated in the era of Augustus. The atrium is especially stately; with its four columns it is considered Pompeii's finest tetrastyle. Opposite the atrium is the tablinum and, to the left, the triclinium opening onto the peristyle. To the right of the atrium: the service wing with kitchen, « calidarium » and « tepidarium », dressing-room, « frigidarium » pool, and lastly the summer triclinium. The peristyle portico, towards the tablinum, is higher and gives the whole complex a monumental originality. At the back of the peristyle is an « exedra » in which the walls have a yellow background; at the sides, two rooms beautifully decorated in the Second Style with architectural panels. In the corner to the left side of the peristyle is a graceful « hoecus tetrastylus » with four small columns covered by a vault; on the walls are more Second Style decorations. Towards the south, the house opens onto an even larger peristyle with an open-air triclinium.

48 The **Gambling House** (Reg. VI, Ins. XIV, no. 28) is on Via di Stabia immediately after the **House of Laocoon**, which is on the right-hand corner of the crossroads. This was a gambling house frequented by both the young men and women of Pompeii. A sign consisting of a vase between two phalluses clearly indicated the entrance. Still written on the walls are the owner's profits from the gambling and the hospitality offered in the rooms on the upper floor. After it comes a **Fullonica** (Ins. XIV, nos. 22 and 21), again converted from a patrician house of which only the atrium is left. Next comes the **House of Orpheus** (Ins. XIV, no. 20), at one time the property of Vesonius Primus and so called because of the large painting depicting Orpheus among the wild beasts which dominated the wall at the back of the peristyle.

49 The **House of L. Caecilius Jucundus** (Reg. IV, Ins. I, no. 26) is opposite the House of Orpheus. Here a strong-box was found still full of books and wax tablets, constituting the banker's records. In the atrium can be seen the bust of the owner (the original, exceptionally powerful and expressive, is in Naples) with its dedication: « Genio L(ucii) nostri Felix l(ibertus) ». To the left of the entrance is the Lararium; around it was sculpted the scene showing the Temple of Jupiter, the Arch and Porta Vesuvius, with the « Castellum aquae » that collapsed during the earthquake in 62 A.D. At the bottom of the tablinum one cas still see traces of some very fine Third Style decorations.

50 The **House of the Young Bull** (Ins. I, no. 7) can be found by turning left on Via di Nola. It is built from blocks of tuff and still retains its Samnite simplicity and severity. The entranceway had a second door to the left so as to block the view of the inside of the house from the street. The wall at the end of the peristyle is interesting with its stuccoed windows and rooms, creating the front of a

House of Lucretius Fronto. Below: Narcissus at the Spring (left) and the Triumph of Bacchus.

nymphaeum; from the three niches, adorned with glass paste and seashells, water once ran down in a graceful series of cascades.

51 The **House of Queen Margaret** (Ins. II, no. 1) has interesting paintings in the rooms at the sides of the tablinum. In the room on the left: Leda and the Swan, Neptune and Amymone, Marsyas and Olympus, Jupiter and Danae, Meleager and Atalanta; in the one on the right: Narcissus, Ariadne, the madness of Lycurgus. Next to this house is the **House of the Triclinium,** named after the banquet scene painted on its wall.

52 The **HOUSE OF M. LUCRETIUS FRONTO** (Ins. IV, no. 11) is reached by turning up the second alley to the left. It is the most interesting and refined among the small « domus » from the Imperial age, with its exquisite paintings in the Third Style. It has been excellently preserved, which helps create an atmosphere of intimacy and serenity. In the tablinum can be seen a Triumph of Bacchus and the Marriage of Venus and Mars (this painting almost seems to be a scene from Pompeian family life). In the room to the right: Narcissus at the Spring and Pero nursing his old father. In the winter triclinium: Orestes slaying Neoptolemus, Theseus and Ariadne, the Toilet of Venus. At the back of the garden is a large African landscape with plants and animals.

Following page: portion of the Via Stabiana.

House of Lucretius Fronto:
Marriage of Venus and Mars painted in the tablinum

House of Obelius Firmus: atrium tetrastylus.

53 The **Barracks of the Gladiators** (Ins. V, no. 3), also on Via di Nola, was a house originally used as a « hospitium » for the « familiae gladiatorum » hired by the city authorities for the displays in the amphiteatre. Graffitti celebrating the gladiators' victories and loves can still be read on the stucco of the columns.

54 The **Porta Nola** is at the end of the street. In the necropolis outside, to the left, worth visiting is the **Sepulchre of Aesquillia Polla**, which is in the form of an « exedra » with a column in the centre holding a burial urn. Recent excavations have uncovered part of the old walls and the tomb of M. Obelius Firmus, who held the offices of aedile and duumvir in Pompeii.

55 The **HOUSE OF M. OBELIUS FIRMUS** (Reg. IX, Ins. IX, nos. 2-4), almost opposite the Barracks of the Gladiators, is a large house begun in the Samnite period. It has two entranceways, the main one on the left leading to the large tetrastyle atrium. In the atrium: marble table, strong-box, fountain with satyr, and in the corner, a small, temple-shaped lararium. At the back is the entrance to an irregular three-sided portico and a large garden. The right wing of the house contains all the service areas. In the tablinum, the large « oecus » of the peristyle and other rooms can be found in-

teresting Second Style paintings, including a medallion with portraits of Obelius's, son and his wife. Note the delightful banquet scene sketched in on the left of the household lararium. Three stairways, one in each atrium and one in the peristyle, led to the upper floor. This floor covered almost the whole ground-floor area and had a row of windows facing onto the garden.

56 The **HOUSE OF THE CENTENARY** (Ins. VI, nos. 3-6) is along the same side of the street, in the direction of the Forum. It was given this name because it was excavated in 1879, the 18th centenary of the tragic eruption. It is a stately dwelling obtained from the union of three earlier homes. Again we have two large atriums, of which the one to the right (Tuscan) still preserves the mosaic floor and traces of small theatrical scenes on the walls. These Fourth Style decorations are also in the « oeci », the rooms off the tablinum, with a white background in the one on the right and a black background in the one to the left. Tablinum: on the walls are great yellow panels with the symbols of Juno, Apollo and Minerva. Next to the pool in the centre of the garden is a copy of the fine « Satyr with Wine-skin ». At the end is an originally open-air nymphaeum, with a niche-type fountain decorated with paintings of plants and birds, fish-ponds and battles between wild beasts. In the smaller part of

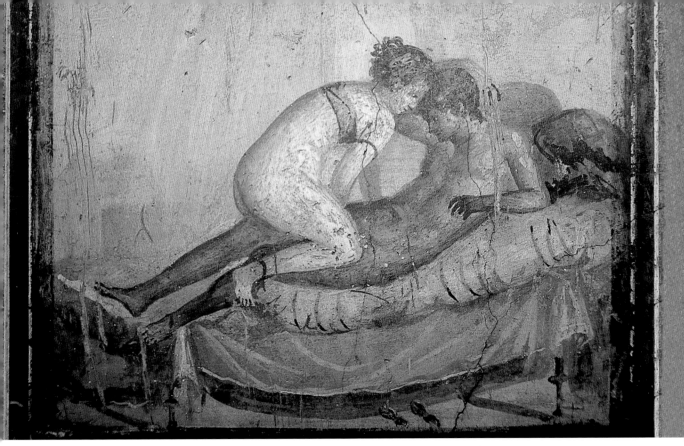

House of the Centenary, detail of a fresco;
below: well-preserved remains of mill stones and ovens.

the house are the secondary atrium with lararium, a bathroom and a group of rooms including one adorned with three panels on a black background.

57 With **Vicolo del Panettiere** we enter the area which was the oldest and least reputable part of Pompeii. On the right is the **House of M. Spurius Mesor** (Reg. VII, Ins. III, no. 29) with paintings done in the Third Style (some now in Naples). On the other side: the **House of Gavius Rufus** (no. 16), of **C. Vibius** (no. 18) and of **Popidius Priscus** (no. 29).
On the corner is the **Pistrinum of Vicolo Storto** (Ins. II, no. 22), probably owned by Popidius Priscus, one of the most typical bakeries, of which there are many in this area (see also the **Pistrinum of Via Stabia, corner of Via degli Augustali**: Reg. IX, Ins. III, nos. 10, 11) with its well-preserved millstones and ovens.
Undoubtedly these bakeries played an important part in Pompeii's business life, supplying nearby towns too with bread, since there were too many of them for the needs of the city alone. Thanks to the material left in the shops and narrative paintings, we can reconstruct the whole production cycle of the bakeries, from the arrival of grain to the sale of their products.

RECONSTRUCTION OF THE ENTIRE WORK CYCLE IN A MILL AND BAKERY ("PISTRINUM") OF TWO THOUSAND YEARS AGO.

To the right at top can be seen the stacking of grain and a man pouring wheat into a large mill driven by an ox. Each mill consists of two stones cut of volcanic rock: one which is solid and conical ("meta"), set on a round masonry base, and the other which is hollow and biconical ("catillus") and rotates on the first. In the lower part of the reconstruction the assembly of a mill is shown: near it, towards the centre, grain is shown being poured into the upper hole, along with the wooden clamp fixed to the neck of the "catillus". Next are two men who turn the "catillus" around so that the wheat descends and is gradually crushed between the two stones until it emerges as flour, at the bottom, being collected in the lead box around the fixed masonry base.
At top left, we can see the dough being made and kneaded (for this purpose metal moulds were used), the most common shape being rings. In the centre we see the oven. After being baked, the various types and shapes of bread were displayed on shelves and counters for sale directly to the public (in the left hand corner of the reconstruction is a scene depicting the sale of bread taken from a painting now in the museum in Naples). Some of the bread made was sent out to the various retailers and to nearby towns.

Above: bakery ("pistrinum") of Via Stabia,
corner of Via degli Augustali;
below: entrance to the Central Baths.

58 The **Central Baths** are found at the intersection between Via di Nola and Via di Stabia, main streets of the city, respectively the « decumanus superior » and « cardo maximus ». Construction of the baths was begun immediately after the earthquake in 62 A.D. in order to meet the growing needs of the new « elite » class of citizens for a meeting place in a fast-recovering city. They were built following the example of the most up-to-date baths in Rome itself, letting in more light to the rooms and creating more space in the open. The facilities were also increased, including a « laconicum », a room even hotter than the « calidarium », used for « sudatio » (sweating). A section for women was not found, but it must be remembered that in 79 the swimming pool had not even been completed nor had the gymnasium been started. On the corner and along Via di Stabia there is a series of large shops and the « **Ubani offectoris** » **Workshop** (Ins. III, no. 2), with its three huge furnaces and boilers in the atrium of a house, used for dyeing fabric.

59 The **House of M. Lucretius** (Ins. III, no. 5) is next to the workshop. This house was the sumptuous dwelling of the priest of Mars and decurion of the city. The atrium was probably completely covered and therefore had no impluvium; to

*Above: small hanging garden in the House
of Marcus Lucretius; below: fountain of the peristyle
in the House of the Bear.*

the right of the atrium is the lararium. Many of the paintings which once adorned the walls are now in Naples, but in the house we can see: mock architectural features in the Fourth Style in the atrium; panels depicting myths, divinities and cupids in the rooms surrounding the atrium; the Triumph of Bacchus, followed by a Satyr and a Victory in the tablinum. In the service wing to the left are the rooms occupied by the kitchen, bakery and latrine. Particularly interesting is the small hanging garden which creates a backdrop to the whole house, while standing out against the circular marble pool is a graceful niche. Once satyrs, cupids and animals frolicked among the flowers, but unfortunately these little statues have either been stolen or placed in safe-keeping.

60 The **HOUSE OF THE BEAR** (Reg. VII, Ins. II, no. 45), on Via degli Augustali, takes its name from the mosaic in the entrance. At the back is a lovely fountain of coloured mosaic and seashells: against its delicate blue mosaic some exquisite figures stand out, including the Floating Venus, small winged figures, little heads and a shoal of darting fish.
Opposite the House of the Bear is the shop of a cobbler (« sutor »), who may also have been the watchman (« ostiarius ») for the house next door.

Painting in the triclinium in the House of Siricus:
Neptune and Apollo present at the construction
of the walls of Troy.

61 The **Inn of Sittius** (Ins. I, nos. 44-45) is along Vicolo del Lupanare, immediately after the House of Mars and Venus. Although it has two entrances, this « hospitium » must have been rather small since its triclinium could contain barely nine people.

The **Brothel** (Ins. XII, no. 18) is on the corner, opposite the inn. The ground floor, with its almost lightless « cellae meretriciae » (prostitutes' rooms), has many obscene paintings and graffitti. The rooms on the upper floor were reached via an independent stairway (no. 20) and by the access gallery projecting over the alley.

62 The **House of the Hanging Balcony** (Ins. XII, no. 28) is where the first balcony in Pompeii was discovered. Next is the **Inn on Vicolo di Eumachia** (nos. 34-35), the most typical of those discovered so far, with its large covered atrium, used as a dining room; to the sides were the bedrooms and kitchen. A small access area led to the stables. Here also the walls are covered with graffitti immortalizing the thoughts of the hotel's clients two thousand years ago.

63 The **House of Siricus** (Ins. I, no. 25, 47) is reached by returning along Vicolo del Lupanare. This house has another entrance on Via di Stabia since it consisted of two connecting homes in which lived two brothers Siricus and Nummianus. There is no doubt that they belonged to well-to-do people: on the entrance to the house on the Vicolo is written « Salve lucrum » (welcome, earnings), a common greeting in Pompeii during the city's last years, when all its citizens were intent on getting rich. In the triclinium are depicted: Neptune and Apollo at the building of the Walls of Troy, Hercules drunk at the court of Omphale, Thetis in Vulcan's workshop.

In the house on Via di Stabia is a lovely atrium with a table, with well-made supports (« trapezophorons »). In the « oecus » are representations of Orestes and Pylades, Mars and Venus, Diana and Endymion; in the triclinium graceful scenes with Cupids.

Continuing along Via Stabia we find « tabernae » of all kinds, among them some small dwellings. At no. 10 is the **Taberna Attiorum**, with a well-preserved room covered by a vault and decorated in the Fourth Style.

64

The **STABIAN BATHS** have the main entrance on Via dell'Abbondanza to the left of the crossroads. They are the largest, best-preserved and the oldest baths, since they were built as soon as the Romans entered Pompeii. The entire complex gravitates around the large trapezoidal peristyle (one can see the tuff columns from the Samnite-Republican period, covered with a thick layer of plaster during the Imperial age). The eastern part was occupied by the men's bathing area with, to a smaller extent, the women's sections and the heating plant in the middle. The men's dressing-room is covered by a vault decorated with beautiful stuccos from the Flavian era (cupids, trophies and bacchants). In the largest area we can see the marble benches and niches for clothing. All the other rooms have the typical shape already found in the small Baths of the Forum. The most important innovation during the Imperial age was in the gymnasium equipment. Here swimming could be alternated with athletic exercises and various different sports. Around the large pool, apart from the dressing-rooms, there were areas where men put oil and sand on their bodies before boxing and cleaned off sweat with the strigil, a spoon-like device. In the portico opposite is a bust of Mercury, god of the gymnasium. On the western walls there are still vast sections of the rich decorations in coloured stuccos with imitation architecture and figures (partly visible, on the door, Jupiter with a sceptre and eagle and on a pillar, Hercules and Satyr).

In the enormous recess is the open-air pool measuring 13 by 8 metres (31 by 25 ft) and 1.5 metres (4 ft) deep. On the sides the lead pipes that carried water to the pool can still be seen. The women's area had two completely independent entrances; their tub for cold baths was in the dressing-room itself. Between the two calidariums serving the mens's and women's sections is the heating plant where the furnace and the three big cylindrical boilers (one for warm, one for hot and one for very hot water) can still be seen.

LAYOUT OF THE STABIAN BATHS

PALAESTRA FACILITIES. 1) *Private entrances.* **2)** *Pool wash basins.* **3)** *Swimming pool.* **4)** *Pool dressing-room.* **5)** *Service area.* **6)** *Entrance and single baths.* **7)** *Latrines.*
MEN'S SECTION. 8) *Entrance.* **9)** *Waiting room.* **10)** *Dressing room and cloak-room.* **11)** *" FRIGIDARIUM ".* **12)** *" TEPIDARIUM ".* **13)** *" CALIDARIUM ".* **14)** *" LACONICUM " (area with a high temperature, like a modern sauna).* **15)** *Entrance to general facilities and furnaces for water and air at various temperatures.* **WOMEN'S SECTION. 16)** *Entrances.* **17)** *Dressing room and tub for cold bath.* **18)** *" TEPIDARIUM ".* **19)** *" CALIDARIUM ".* **20)** *Ambulatory.*

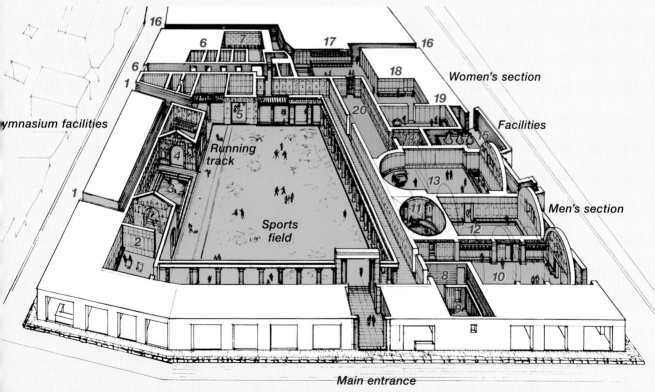

Gymnasium facilities · Running track · Sports field · Women's section · Facilities · Men's section · Main entrance

Stabian Baths. Above: large square in the open-air palestra; below: detail of the "frigidarium".

Stabian Baths. Above: dressing room ("apodyterium") with bench and niches for clothing; below: cast of a victim of the eruption of 79 A.D. on exhibit in the dressing room.

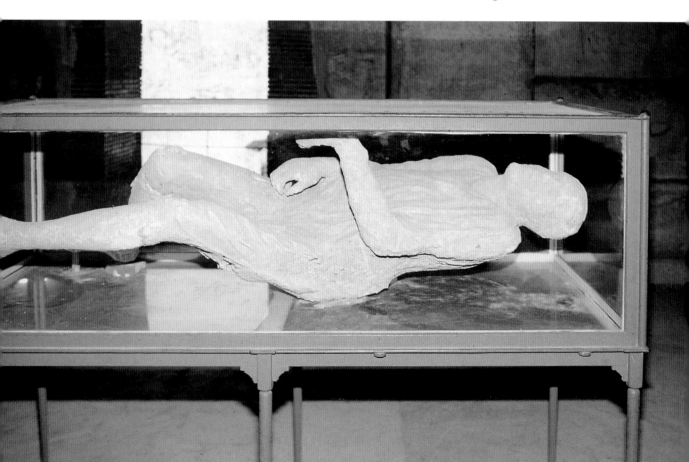

65 The **Crossroads** formed by the main streets **Via di Stabia** (« cardo maximus ») and **Via dell'Abbondanza** (lower « decumanus maximus ») is the most important in the city. To the east are one of the pillars used for raising water and distributing it to the area and the public fountain. Along Via dell'Abbondanza, which becomes much wider near the Forum, are the remains of the four pillars on which an arch with four openings rested; against each pillar were statues in honour of various citizens, including one of M. Holconius Rufus who restored and enlarged the Large Theatre during the Roman era.

66 The **House of M. Epidius Rufus** (Ins. I, no. 20) is to the left of the crossroads along Via dell'Abbondanza. A sign of exceptional distinction was the fact that the house stood on a high podium (1.5 metres or some four ft above street level), and the main entrance door was opened only on special occasions. The atrium is one of the most grandiose in Pompeii and had no less than 16 columns (polystyle) measuring 4.5 metres (over 14 ft) high. To the sides of the atrium are two areas that have columns with figured Corinthian capitals at the entrance. On the lararium is a dedication from two freedmen to the owner and household gods: « Genio Marci nostri et Laribus· ». At the end of the atrium, passing through the tablinum, we reach the triclinium which has traces of interesting paintings: mock architecture and stylized plants, a scene depicting Marsyas challenging Apollo to a flute-playing contest before the Muses.

*Crossroads where Via Stabia
and Via dell'Abbondanza meet.*

67 The **House of Cornelius Rufus** (Reg. VIII, Ins. IV, no. 15), opposite the Baths, had belonged to the « gens Cornelia » ever since the age of Sulla. The portrait of the owner, at one time in the tablinum, can now be seen in the Antiquarium. The trapezophorons (supports for the marble table) at the edge of the impluvium are superb. Alongside this house is the **House of a barber** (no. 12) and then a **Laundry** belonging to a person named **Gelon** (no. 9).

68 The **House of Holconius Rufus** (Ins. IV, no. 4) is at the other end of the block opposite the Baths. This was the dwelling of the man who was the tribune, duumvir and priest of Augustus, patron of the colony, whose statue could be found at the important nearby crossroads. Traces still remain of the rich decorations (mask of Oceanus, Silenus holding the young Bacchus) that were once on the walls. Figures of bacchants and various mythological scenes can be seen in some rooms. The summer triclinium has a fountain and paintings which have almost completely disappeared. In the room to the left are depicted Orestes, Pylades and Iphigenia; in the one to the right Europa, Nereid on a dolphin and a god.

69 The **TRIANGULAR FORUM** is behind the House of Holconius. This forum, taking its name from the unusual shape of the land available for it, occupies only one third of Pompeii's second large civic centre.

The entrance, to the north, has a portico (propylaeum) with six elegant Ionic columns and with two shelves at the sides for night lamps. The square is surrounded on two sides by a portico of 95 Doric columns; on the east side it is connected to the Palaestra, the Large Theatre and, via a long flight of steps, to the Arcaded Court. The base near the front portico was for a statue of Marcus Claudius Marcellus, patron of Pompeii and favourite nephew of the Emperor Augustus.

The **Doric Temple**, which occupies the southern area, was built in the 6th century B.C., when Pompeii was under the Greek influence of the powerful State of Cumae. It was consecrated to Hercules, mythical founder of the city, and later included also the cult of Minerva. It was reconstructed several times in the Samnite period, but was almost abandoned during the Roman age. The temple was quite similar to the ones built at the same time at Paestum: it had sturdy, wide-fluted columns with wide, very flat capitals, the columns completely surrounding the cella (peripteral). There were 32 columns in all, with seven columns on the two smaller facades (that is with a column in the middle). Almost the whole building was made of tuff, only the columns (of which we can still see some fragments) being made of limestone from Sarno. The base is well-preserved (about 21 × 28 metres, or 67 × 90 ft) with its narrow stairway to the south.

In front of the main entrance to the temple, the one facing nearly east, there are remains of the shrine dedicated to Hercules, with two altars on the right. Further on we can see what is left of the sacred well once covered by a small, circular temple with eight slender columns, built by the Samnite N. Trebius. Behind the temple is a semi-circular bench where the duumvirs placed a sun-dial, the same duumvirs responsible for the similar sun-dial in front of the Temple of Apollo.

70 The **Samnite Palaestra** was built by the duumvir Vibius Vinicius for young Samnites. It has a portico on three sides, with facilities to the west. Votive wreaths offered by winners of competitions to Mercury, the god of athletic games, were placed on the table.

Monumental entranceway (propilaeums) to the Triangular Forum.

71 The **LARGE THEATRE**, built so as to fit into a great curve in the sloping ground, dates from the end of the 3rd century B.C. During the Augustan era it was enlarged and adapted to meet new needs by the architect M. Artorius on behalf of the Holconii family. Dating from this period are the « crypta » (covered corridor) with its « summa cavea », that is, the upper seating area, and the « tribunalia », the boxes built over the side entrances and reserved for priestesses and the person presiding over the performance. These seats were added to the « media cavea », 15 steps divided into five sections, and the « ima cavea », which was the lowest part with seats reserved for the most important citizens. During the city's last years, even the « orchestra », meaning the semi-circular pit in front of the stage, was occupied by prominent Pompeians,

and the theatre could thus seat more than 5000 people. Between the stage and the orchestra is a long opening where the curtain was gathered up once the performance began. The two wide entrances to the sides of the stage were used for large theatrical displays. The Roman stage (built over the Greek-type stage, which consisted of a simple backdrop with two projecting structures) has a monumental facade adorned with columns, cornices, pediments, statues and water gushing from fountains. It must have been very similar to the mock architecture painted in the Fourth Style. The large seating area was completely protected from the sun and rain by an enormous canopy (« velarium ») held up by poles fastened in rings that can still be seen at the back of the top seating area. The theatre itself was built of stone, only the stage being brickwork.

The seats and stage in the Large Theatre
as they appear today.

The stage in the Large Theatre as it was in the 1st century A.D.. Note the canopy ("velarium") extended over the theatre to protect the spectators from the rain and sun. The large immovable stage seems to give concrete form to the mock architecture painted in the Fourth Style.

Aerial view of the area occupied by the Triangular Forum and the theatres, as it is today.

RECONSTRUCTION OF THE AREA OCCUPIED BY THE TRIANGULAR FORUM AND THE THEATRES

Top right, we see the complex of the Triangular Forum and the theatres as they appeared at the beginning of the 1st century A.D. On the left of the reconstruction the Triangular Forum stands out with the Greek temple from the 6th century B.C. In front of the temple, dedicated to Hercules, there are a small enclosure with cells and a sacred cistern, over which is built a round shrine ("tholos") with eight little columns. At the top we see the smaller ancient Samnite palaestra; the shrine of the Mysteries of Isis; and the temple of Jupiter Meilichios. The Large Theatre is in the centre of the reconstruction, with the poles around the top on which the canopy was raised. At the bottom we see the square mass of the small Theatre, solidly covered by its pyramid-shaped roof. Entrances to the theatres were from the Forum via a long stairway, from Via di Stabia via long galleries or directly from the street. In front of the theatres was the great Arcaded Court once thronged by spectators and later enlarged by Nero, who had rooms and facilities built on the two floors to convert it into living quarters for the gladiators.

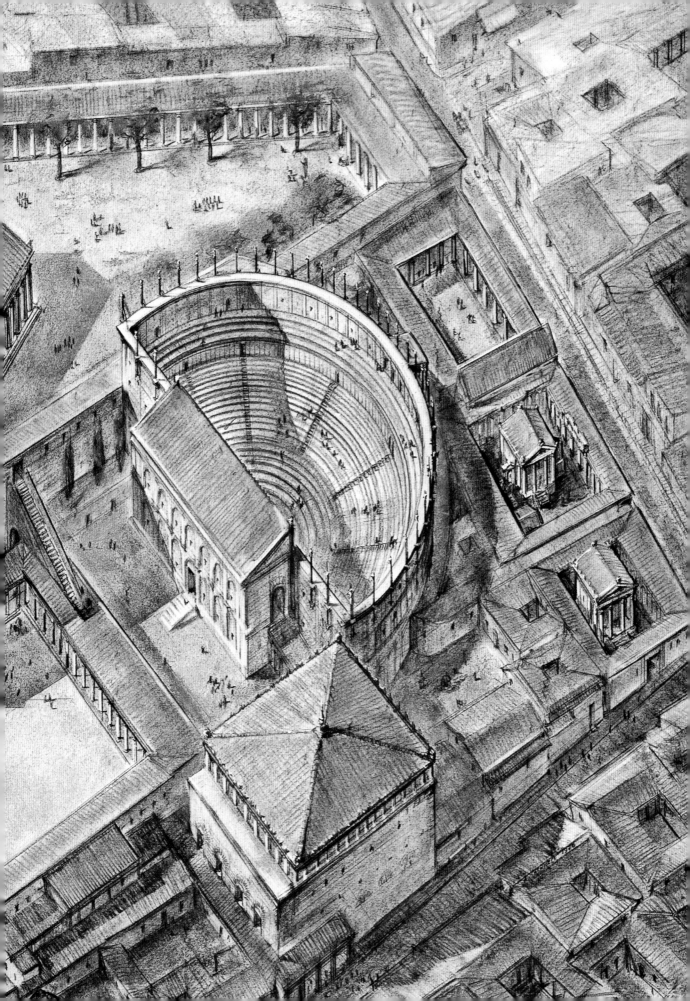

Small Theatre. Above: the seating area and stage;
left: detail of the sculpted tuff "telamone" at the end
of the parapet.

72 The **SMALL THEATRE** is one of the most perfect examples of a roofed theatre (« theatrum tectum »), that is, an « Odeon » which in ancient times was used for musical performances and mime. It was built in 80 B.C. by the duumvirs C. Quitius Valgus and M. Porcius. The « summa » and the « media cavea » (top and central seating) have 17 steps made from tuff, while the « ima cavea » (lowest seating) has four; on the sides are two parapets with two statues of tuff (telamones) at the ends. The seats for the decurions were distinguished by the winged lion's claws on their sides. The great block of brickwork at the end of most of the cavea steps supported an imposing pyramid-shaped roof which probably had a double ceiling on the inside.

73 The **Arcaded Court** connected to the theatres is behind the large stage and was originally a colonnaded square (« porticus post scaenam ») where the theatre-goers met before the performance and during the intermissions. During the age of Nero it was transformed into a barracks for the ever-increasing number of gladiators engaged for the contests in the amphitheatre. The rooms ran all around the court on the two floors, and on the east side were the refectory and kitchen. Fine examples of weapons (now in Naples) were found in the barracks.

Right: entrance halls in the Small Theatre;
below: the great Arcaded Court where gladiators lived.

The Temple of Isis and its sacred enclosure as seen today.

74 The **TEMPLE OF ISIS** is next to the Samnite palaestra and is entered by the street named after it, Via d'Iside. It was dedicated to the worship of the goddess from the Egyptian triad, a cult which was spreading throughout the Roman Empire. After its destruction in the earthquake of 62, the temple was rebuilt by N. Popidius Celsinus, who was elected decurion despite the fact that he was only six years old. The high walls around the consecrated area hid from view the sacred mysteries that took place within. The temple, facing east, stood on a tall podium completely dominating the small open area round it. It had an atrium with six columns (two on each side and four along the front); in the short, open cella were the sacred instruments and symbols of the cult of Isis. Two structures with niches for statues and images of the goddess projected from the sides of the cella. The main altar was beside the steps, and to the north was another altar which contained the remains of a sacrifice. Behind the temple is a room where the initiates met. On the south side are the priests' rooms; on the corner is a small temple decorated with stuccos from which a passage leads to the cistern which contained the sacred water of the Nile. This building, without the paintings, statues and images it once had, gives an even greater sense of melancholy and mystery.

75 The **Temple of Jupiter Meilichios** is on Via di Stabia. It dates from pre-Roman times and was originally used for the worship of « Zeus Meilichios », a cult brought from Grecian Sicily. It has six columns in the pronaos, like the Temple of Isis, but had a deeper cella built from tuff. Also of tuff is the interesting large altar in front of the steps. After the earthquake in 62 had destroyed the Temple of Jupiter in the Forum, this smaller temple was adapted to the worship of the Capitoline triad; in fact, two large statues in terracotta of Jupiter and Juno and a bust of Minerva have been found here (National Museum of Naples).

The Temple of Isis with the sacred enclosure and the shrine for the sacred water of the Nile (at left) as they were two thousand years ago.

76 The **Porta Stabia** is at the end of Via di Stabia, just past the covered theatre. This gate still has the great blocks of limestone from the Samnite period. The deep ruts testify to the heavy traffic that used this important road, linking the heart of Pompeii to the port, the most wealthy villages (« pagi ») and important towns to the south of the Gulf of Naples. On the outside is another **Necropolis** in which there are two tombs with the typical semi-circular seat (« scholae »); the first belongs to Marcus Tullius, who had the Temple of Fortuna Augusta built, the second to the duumvir M. Alleius Minius.

77 The **House of the Citharist** (Ins. IV, no. 5) can be found by returning along Via di Stabia, near Via dell'Abbondanza. It is one of Pompeii's largest aristocratic homes, created by uniting two already spacious houses. It has three peristyles on several levels, and in the central one was found the beautiful bronze statue of Apollo Citharoedus, now in Naples. Also in Naples are the paintings that adorned the walls. In fact, all that is left in the actual house are faded traces of what was probably one of the wealthiest homes in Pompeii. However, its architectural layout is interesting, as is the bathing area by the first atrium, with its tepidarium and calidarium supplied with water from the furnace in the adjacent kitchen.

Turning west along Via dell'Abbondanza one enters the zone of the new excavations (begun in 1911). Here skillful and experienced workers, using new methods which are being perfected continually, have reached new heights in the techniques of excavation work, making it possible to bring back to life what has been preserved under the ashes for 1900 years. This is why the whole zone, despite the damage done by bombings in 1943 and by the ravages of time (and tourists), appears completely different from what we have seen so far. Besides the fascination of the interiors, there is particular interest in the exterior of the buildings, a picturesque series which stretches uninterrupted along Via dell'Abbondanza. In keeping with the stage reached in the excavation works, we feel it is best to give an overall picture of this street, with its exteriors, before considering the other more interesting buildings in the area.

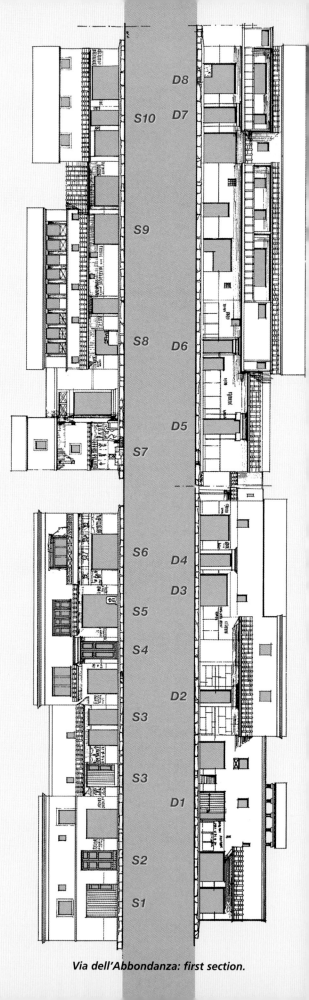

Via dell'Abbondanza: first section.

VIA DELL'ABBONDANZA

The longitudinal drawings on this and on pages 86 and 87 are reconstructions of the street fronts in the sections brought to light by recent excavations. Together with the reconstructions on pages 97 and 109, they give us a complete picture of one of the main streets of Pompeii, a street that was full of life, with a touch of colour added by the writings and small paintings on the façades of the houses, as well as the jumble of different shapes and sizes of the balconies, loggias, and roofs projecting over the street. Not much is left of this, but the various elements recovered in the excavations, which have become increasingly precise since the beginning of this century, permit accurate reconstructions to be made.

The numbers shown on the drawings indicate the objects of major interest to the left (S) and to the right (D) of the road; in the text the data and numbers given on the monuments are also indicated.

FIRST SECTION

Region IX. Insula VII. - S. 1 (n° 10) "Taberna" with marks left by the wooden locks (there were similar devices for closing all the shops, consisting of a normal bascule-type door which had vertical sliding staves, the whole apparatus being locked into place by a long bolt). S. 2 (n° 9) House of Popidius Montanus, with upper floor used for meetings of the "latrunculari", the chess players of the time. On the exterior are electoral writings. S. 3 (n° 7-5) workshop of M. Vecilius Verecundus in which wool garments and felt were made ("coactilia"). At sides of door n° 7: Mercury coming out of a shrine with a sack of money, Venus Pompeiana on an elephant-drawn chariot escorted by cupids and Lares; underneath are depicted the weaving, dyeing and sale of the woollen goods. S. 4 (n° 3) House of the Sittii with a cast of the door. Even the large doors in residential buildings were very similar: two tall leaves with a cross-type frame and often embellished with bronze studs. S. 6 (n° 1) "Taberna" of the Four Gods painted on the architrave: Apollo-Sun, Jupiter, Mercury, Diana-Moon. To the left of the door: Venus Pompeiana with cupids, to the right: traces of a sacred procession and a niche for a bearded Bacchus.

Region I, Insula VII. - D. 1 (n ° 7) Fullonica Stephani. Cast of the long bolt and lock (see page 100 for the interior). D. 2 (n° 4) House of the Lararium (see page 101). D. 3 (n° 3) Emporium of Verus, "faber aerarius", manufacturer and seller of bronze furnishings and tools among which was found a "groma" (surveyor's square now in the museum). D. 4 (n° 2) House of the Cryptoporticus (see page 101).

Region IX. Insula XI - S. 7 Public shrine ("compitum") with paintings of the place's twelve protecting gods. S. 8 (n° 2) Thermopolium of Asellina which sold hot beverages. It was found complete with all

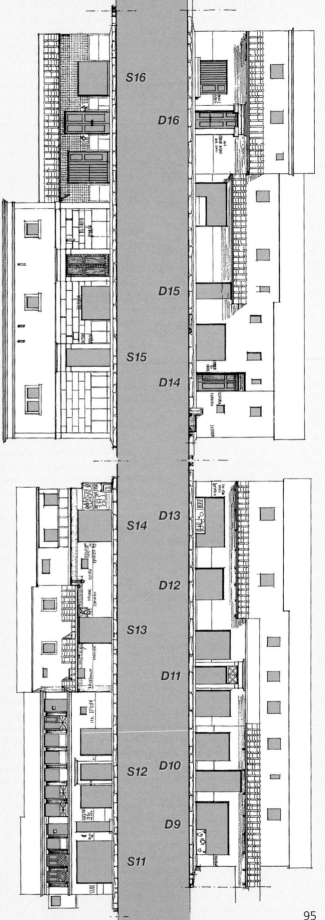

Via dell'Abbondanza: second section.

Preceding page, top: a section of Via dell'Abbondanza, in the foreground the public shrine of the place's twelve protecting gods; bottom: the interior of the Thermopolium of Asellina with the lararium on the end wall.

Via dell'Abbondanza as it was in the section between the "Taberna" with the four gods and the "Taberna" with sign of the vases (see page 94, between S. 6 and S. 9). On the left, under the large balcony with pergola, are the painted heads of four household gods. In the centre is the shrine dedicated to the twelve gods who protected the area. Past the elegant entrance of a house is the Thermopolium of Asellina and, to the right at the end, the tavern with the sign showing metal vases for choice wines.

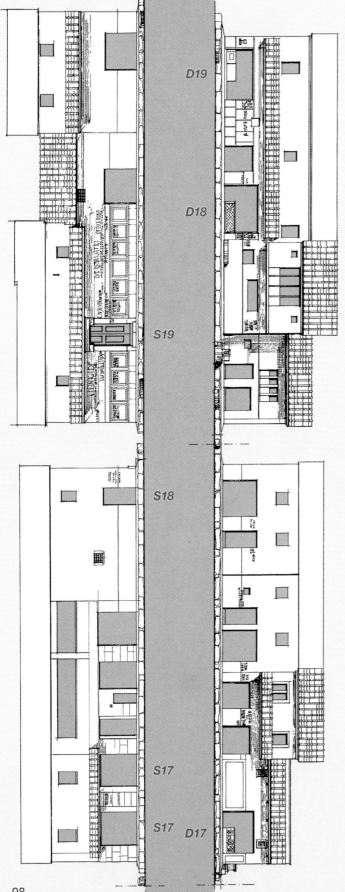

its equipment, lamps, records of accounts and a boiler that was still hermetically sealed. The foreign names of the girls Aegle, Maria, Smyrna and Asellina, who were available on the upper floor, were written on the wall. S. 9 (n° 4). "Taberna" with its painted sign consisting of large metal containers full of wine. S. 10 (n° 7) Traces of paintings of Minerva Sacrificing.

Region I. Insula VII - D. 5 (n° 1) House of P. Paquius Proculus (see page 103). From the writings on the walls, he seems to have been the most active political figure in the area. D. 6 (n°s 2-3) House of Fabius Amandio (see page 104). D. 7 (n° 7) House of the Priest Amandus (see page 105). D. 8 (n° 8) Thermopolium.

SECOND SECTION

Region IX. Insula XII. - S. 11 (n° 2) House of the First Cenaculum (large loggia on upper level). S. 12 (n°s. 3-5) House of the Second Cenaculum (large loggia on the upper level with small tuff columns and pillars) and textile workshops ("Textrinae"). S. 13 (n° 6) "Taberna" of Crescens. To the right, painting of a phallic Mercury. S. 14 (n° 7) House of C. Maximus. On the corner of the alley, "compitum" with painting of "Genio Augusti".

Region I. Insula XIII - D. 9 (n° 1) "Taberna pomaria" which sold fruit. Counter painted with bachant motifs. D. 10 (n°s 2-3) House and "Taberna" of Stephanus. D. 11 (n° 5) House where a small Indian statue was found, evidence of trade with Alexandria in Egypt and with India. D. 12 (n° 7) House and bakery of Betutius Justus. D. 13 (n° 8) "Taberna" with three sales counters and a lararium with paintings of Mercury and Bacchus between the Genius loci (local divinity) and the Lares.

Region IX. Insula XIII. - S. 15 (n° 1-3) House of C. Julius Polybius. Samnite façade with perfect rustication, with beautiful portals and a cornice. S. 16 (n°s. 4-5-6) House and Fullonica of Fabius Ulutremulus. Façade in polychrome checkerboard design. Beside the door at n° 5 are traces of small paintings: Aeneas fleeing from Troy and Romulus with the trophy of Acron. At the right of n° 4, a sad and prophetic poem that begins:"nihil durare potest tempore perpetuo...", (nothing can last forever....).

Region I. Insula IX - D. 14 (n° 1) House of the Beautiful Impluvium (see page 106). Cast of the door (entrance is from the "taberna" at n° 2) and frescoed "protyron" depicting six household gods: Venus, Minerva, Juno, Bacchus, Hercules and Mercury. D. 15 (n° 3) House of Successus (see page 106). D. 16 (n° 5) House of the Orchard (see page 106). Today the entrance is at n° 6.

Via dell'Abbondanza: third section.

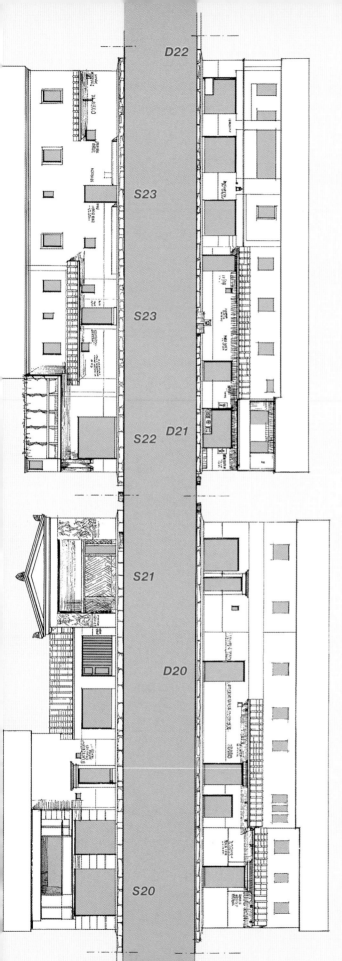

THIRD SECTION

Region III. Insula I. - S. 17 (n° 1-2) " Tabernae" with inscription of the name Cassii Calpurni. S. 18 (n° 6) "Taberna" with the name of Predicius Cornelius.

Region I. Insula XI - D. 17 (n° 1) "Caupona", tavern where workers who made mats, garments etc. assembled ("Tegettari"). On the architrave: shrine with household gods (Penates). Counter with polychrome marble tiles. On the corner of the alley is a public altar and the painting of the serpent "Agathodemon".

Region III. Insula II - S. 19 (n° 1) House of Aulus Trebius Valens (see page 106). The orignal façade, destroyed in the bombings of 1943, was covered with inscriptions; in some of these, Trebius supported candidates in the municipal elections, while in others there were announcements of contests in the arena, giving the names of the pairs of gladiators who would be fighting and stating that the would be covered with the "velarium".

Region I. Insula VII - D. 18 (n° 3) "Caupona" of Setericus (see page 107). To the right is the sign of "Roma". D. 19 (n° 5) "Taberna". To the right the sign "Africa ".

FOURTH SECTION

Region III. Insula III. - S. 20 (n° 1) Workshop of the mat workers, garment workers etc. ("tegettari"). S. 21 (n° 6) "Schola Armaturarum" (see page 107). The façade, partially destroyed in the bombings of 1943, had an unusual feature: a wide doorway was blocked by a low wooden wall of lattice-like structure (faithfully reconstructed) and a triangular pediment at the top. Beside the main door were two large Roman trophies of the Julii (part of the one on the left is still intact).

Region I. Insula XIII - D. 20 (n° 4) "Sutoria Primigenia" (shoe factory).

Region III. Insula IV - S. 22 (n° 1) Pottery "Taberna" of Zosimus, meeting place for the residents of the "Urbulana" Gate. The alley to the left (Vicolo di Ifigenia) is now being excavated so as to connect this area with Porta Nola. Along this "vicolo" is the entrance to the House of Pinarius Cerialis (see page 107). S. 23 (n°s 2-3) House of T. Arrius Polites (or House of the Moralist; see page 107) and House of M. Epidius Hymenaeus. After the block called Insula IV is an alley with writings in which the owners of the buildings invoked the wrath of Jupiter on those who dirtied the walls.

Region II. Insula I - D. 21 (n° 1) Caupona of Hermes with painted counter. At numbers 4, 5 and 6 are three large "tabernae". D. 22 corner of the alley with "Castellum aquae" which still has the lead water tank and the taps at the bottom for regulating intake and output. Next are the blocks of the First Region with three large houses, and then the Forum Boarium (cattle market).

At the Sarno Gate (the ancient Porta Urbulana) is the end of Via dell'Abbondanza, the main street which cuts lengthways through the whole city extending for more than a kilometre.

Via dell'Abbondanza: fourth section.

78 The **FULLONICA STEPHANI** (Reg. I, Ins. VI, no. 7) is one of the largest laundries found up to now and is yet another clear example of the transformation of a private home into a workshop. In the drawing below we have sought to represent the work and commercial cycle as it was in the Fullonica Stephani (as in all the « fullonicae ») in the first half of the 1st century A.D.

Dirty clothes arrived at the back of the fullonica, except for the more delicate clothes which were washed in the former atrium, using the impluvium, transformed into a tub equipped for this purpose (see centre-left). Clothes with more resistant stains were literally trampled by workers in three oval tubs (« saltus fullonici »); then, together with the other clothes, they were placed in larger tubs (see extreme right) and were gradually and carefully cleaned. Sulphur vapour and special ingredients put in the water were used to bleach clothes. Any dyeing was done in special vessels. The proprietress, whose name was Specle, supervised from the middle of this area, which was the most important section of the laundry operations.

Clothes were hung to dry in the the sun on the terraces on the top floor (see top right). Next to the tubs (see lower right) was the combined kitchen and small dining room as well as the latrine for servants. This area was brightened by a small open-air garden in the middle. In the room that was once the triclinium of the house (see centre) the clean clothes were put in order and passed, via a small internal window, into the former « oecus » of the atrium to be ironed and mended. Tunics and togas were ironed with a press called a « thorcular ».

In the same room (see left, above the impluvium) clothes were returned to the customers and those made by the company were displayed and sold. On the right of the vestibule was the checking and cashier's office, probably run by the proprietor himself, Stephanus. In the room near the press was the supervisor who kept an eye on both workers and customers. On the top floor were the living quarters of the owners.

79 The **House of the Lararium** (Ins. VI, no. 4) was being redecorated when Pompeii was destroyed (one can still see the materials that were ready). Under the little vault of the lararium (to the right of the tablinum) is a frieze with white bas-reliefs on a blue background, which is especially interesting. The frieze illustrates, in a series of continuous scenes, the last book of the Iliad: Hector saying farewell and facing Achilles, then his dead body being dragged around the walls of Troy; Priam recovering the body of his son and taking it to Troy. The room to the east of the peristyle, known as the Room of the Elephants, has a fine mosaic floor and traces of a large painting in the Second Style.

80 The **HOUSE OF THE CRYPTOPORTICUS** (Ins. VI, no. 2) belonged to the Valerii Rufi family. In its last years it had been divided into two houses, and the new owner, more interested in commerce than in art, was transforming it into a warehouse. The upper floor has two entrances and two atriums and, in this case, the larger atrium is the one on the left without columns; this whole level is more or less devoid of decorations. The most interesting part, reached by descending a small stairway to the side of the peristyle, is the Cryptoporticus: to the left are all the areas for bathing

House of Ceius Secundus: atrium and hunting scene depicted on a wall of the small garden.

(furnace, calidarium, tepidarium, frigidarium) and at the back is the dining-cum-living room. Note carefully the remaining traces of stuccos and paintings in order to realize how this fine gallery must have looked two thousand years ago, with along the walls a continuous series of herms and caryatids (male and female) in antique yellow marble, like the animated pillars of a portico surmounted by a vault richly decorated with arches and innumerable panels of coloured stucco. A continuous wave of green festoons ran from pillar to pillar. The back wall, done in deep-red panels, was surmounted by a frieze depicting scenes from the Iliad. In the dining-cum-living room (« oecus tricliniaris ») the paintings are still quite visible. The architectural motif is taken up again, and the herms and caryatids become half busts supporting, like red porphyry pillars, the fine cornice (no longer interrupted by windows as in the cryptoporticus) which is embellished with corbels in the shape of bulls in relief (now badly damaged). At the top of the walls, painted bright yellow, between one caryatid and another, are painted mock windows opening onto small, exquisite scenes: among the first of these are cocks and baskets of fruit, and on the left is the best of all, depicting the Marriage of Ariadne.

81 The **House of L. Ceius Secundus** or House of Fabia and Tyrannus (Ins. VI, no 15) is one of the smallest but most exquisite dwellings in Pompeii. The facade, still intact, has a covering of imitation marble stuccos, a small projecting roof over the footpath, wall inscriptions and the cast of the double-leaf door with cross-bar. On the inside is the pleasant atrium with four painted, stuccoed columns; at the back there was an internal stairway and balcony leading to the upper floor; to the left one can see the cast made of a wardrobe. There are interesting and pleasant paintings almost everywhere; on the walls at the back of the small garden is a single large painting depicting scenes of the Nile and hunting scenes framed by rich figured decorations.

At no. 11 is what was perhaps originally the **House of P. Casca Longus**, one of the conspirators who assassinated Caesar. The comic and tragic theatrical scenes painted in the atrium are interesting.

82 The **HOUSE OF MENANDER** (Ins. X, no. 4) is a large wealthy home facing the House of Fabia. It belonged to « Quintus Poppaeus », another relative of the second wife of Nero, Poppaea Sabina. The actual house is in the centre; to the right of the peristyle, the kitchen-bathroom area; to the

House of Menander: peristyle.

left of the peristyle is the large triclinium with its « oeci ». Behind the triclinium are the servants' quarters and beyond are the stable with a courtyard and other facilities and shops around it. To the side of the triclinium are the quarters of the house's administrator (« procurator »). In the atrium are traces of a noteworthy painting in the Fourth Style, with landscapes and hunting scenes; in the corner, a small temple-lararium. In the area which opens to the left of the atrium (« exedra ») are three scenes of the conquest of Troy: Death of Laocoon and his sons; the Trojan Horse and Cassandra; Menelaus, Helen and Cassandra; and Ajax. The decorations in the rooms opening onto the peristyle are interesting, among them the frieze on the walls, with Centaurs and Leucippids and a floor mosaic with Nile scenes. The niches in the walls at the back of the peristyle are full of decorations; note the figure of Menander (a Greek poet almost as famous in the ancient world as Homer) seated with a « volumen » in his left hand. Note also the theatrical masks, hunting scenes with Diana and Actaeon and a small rustic temple with Venus. A small chapel for worshipping the wax busts of ancestors (« imagines maiorum ») was built in the last semi-circular niche. The painted stuccos and mosaics in the « calidarium » to the right of the peristyle are also noteworthy. Found in the house's basement rooms in 1930 were no less than 114 pieces of silverware and numerous precious coins.

83 The **HOUSE OF THE LOVERS** (Ins. X, no 11), in the same block as the House of Menander, is another small but elegant dwelling that is well-preserved. Worthy of interest are the attractive paintings in the atrium, as well as the small internal portico, on two levels, onto which the upper rooms face. An atmosphere of intimacy can still be felt in this house, and perhaps it was the young married couple who were making it their home who wrote on one of the panels of the portico: « amantes ut apes vitam mellitam exigunt » (lovers, like bees, make life as sweet as honey). In the same block are two other small dwellings worth noting: at no. 7, a beautiful table in the atrium and the painting of Daedalus and Icarus; at no. 8, a typical painting, depicting a garden, on the high plinth.

84 The **HOUSE OF PAQUIUS PROCULUS** or of Cuspius Pansa (Ins. VII, no. 1) is reached by returning along Via dell'Abbondanza; it is on the block immediately following that of the Cryptoporticus. This is a small « domus » with a large

Above, left: portrait of Paquius Proculus and his wife, now in the National Museum of Naples.

House of the Priest Amandus. Above: the Flight of Icarus; left: Perseus freeing Andromeda.

Following page: open-air triclinium in the House of Cornelius Tages (or of the Ephebus).

peristyle. The beautiful mosaic pavement extending from the entrance to the tablinum can still be seen: note particularly in the vestibule the figure of a dog tied to a half-open door blocking entry to the house. In the atrium is a great carpet of mosaic with panels depicting animals, two medallions with male busts and the drawing of an arched colonnade around the impluvium. Finally, in the centre of the triclinium is a Nile scene (dwarves in a boat and animals). The garden had facilities for dining in the open. Above the portico was a loggia connected to the top floor. The portrait of Paquius Proculus and his wife, famous for its exceptionally life-like quality, was found in this house and later taken to the National Museum of Naples.

Next is the **House of Fabius Amandio** (Ins. VII, nos. 2-3), a small but dignified dwelling with ingenious architectural solutions which exploit to the full the little available space on the two floors.

85 The **House of the Priest Amandus** (Ins. VII, no. 7) has an interesting series of small paintings in the triclinium (to the right of the atrium). They are in the Third Style and depict, from right to left: Polyphemus as shepherd, Galatea and Ulysses' ship, Perseus freeing Andromeda, Perseus in the palace of King Cepheus, Hercules in the garden of the Hesperides, the flight of Daedalus and Icarus, and Icarus falling into the sea. The peristyle was shaded by a huge tree, of which the marks left by the roots have been found.

86 The **HOUSE OF THE EPHEBUS** or Cornelius Tages (Ins. VII, nos. 11-12) is another example of a dwelling owned by a merchant who had become rich in the last years of Pompeii. To the right of the entrance is the private part of the house in which should be noted: the lararium; the bedroom with black walls, designed for two beds (« bicliniaris ») and with antechamber; and the loggia on the top floor. To the left are the living room and reception rooms. Along the passage which leads to the garden is a handsome room with a mosaic and decorations of darting fish. The floor of the triclinium, to the right, is decorated with delicate designs in coloured marbles and pieces of glass paste; walls and ceiling are covered with decorations and there were once winged figures in gilded stucco at the top. At the back of the portico is a small temple-lararium embellished with white stucco on a blue background. Abutting onto the lararium is a water filter tank (« castellum aquae ») which conveniently hides the large fresco depicting the loves of Mars and Venus. In the garden are the seats of the open-air triclinium sheltered by a pergola supported by four columns (a series of painted panels can be seen inside the podium), and a gushing fountain lent a light, cool touch to the whole scene. At the back is a small stairway which leads to another apartment which was part of the house: the walls of its peristyle are painted with garden scenes, and in the tablinum are paintings of the marriage of Venus and Mars and Hylas and the Nymphs.

House of Trebius Valens: entrance.

87 The **House of the Beautiful Impluvium** (Reg. I, Ins. IX, no. 1) is two blocks further along the street on the south side. This house was also in the process of being rebuilt after the earthquake. Note the impluvium in the atrium with its basin of mosaics and polychrome marbles; in the tablinum are traces of a large painting on black background done in the Second Style; and in the cubiculum is a delightful little painting depicting scenes of the women's quarters.

88 The **House of Successus** (Ins. IX, no. 3) has a graceful painting of a little putto being frightened by a flapping duck, in the room to the left of the atrium; under the painting is written « Successus ». In the small portico, note che charming statue of another little putto with a dove.

89 The **HOUSE OF THE ORCHARD** (Ins IX, no. 5), the last in the block, is the simple, yet elegant dwelling of a fruit grower. In two rooms - one in the atrium on a blue background, the other in the tablinum on a black background - are the finest paintings which depict fruit trees. Along with birds, snakes and other animals, the different fruit which can be identified includes pears, figs, plums, cherries and lemons (very rare in the Campania of those days).

90 The house of **C. Julius Polybius** (Reg. IX, Ins. XVII, nos. 1—5) is on the other side of Via dell'Abbondanza. It was built in the 2nd century B.C., and excavation works, which are still going on, continue to bring parts of it to light. A unique feature of the house is the atrium preceded by a room, poorly lit by slits from the upper floor but with important decorations in the First Style. Two « cubicula » decorated in the Second and Third Styles open onto the atrium. On the top floor: painting of an imitation door on the staircase landing; in a « cubiculum » paintings of Pasiphae and the wooden cow, and Venus and Mars. On an outside wall (no. 4) a wandering poet had scratched four pentameters which began: « nihil durare potest tempore perpetuo... » (nothing can last forever).

91 The **HOUSE OF TREBIUS VALENS** (Reg. IX, Ins. XIX, no. 1) is further ahead on the north side of Via dell'Abbondanza. The facade, unfortunately half destroyed during the bombings of 1943, had an extraordinary collection of writings on the wall about the owner's electoral platform plus advertisements for performances in the Amphitheatre. The inside was excavated after restorations in 1952. The impression one has on entering the atrium is quite out of the ordinary because of the unusual checkered polychrome decoration on the wall at the back of the garden. The paintings in the Third Style, found all over the house, are also very pleasant as are the Second Style architectural paintings in one of the bedrooms. In the garden, against the checkerboard decoration, is the summer triclinium sheltered by a colonnaded pergola and served from the kitchen via a special service-hatch.

The **Pistrinum of Sotericus** (Reg. I, Ins. XII, nos. 1,2) opposite the previous house, is the bakery of Via dell'Abbondanza, one of the largest in the city. Especially intriguing is the dough-mixer which was run by an ingenious mechanism; note how the bread was transferred directly from this area to the oven.

Further along Via dell'Abbondanza is the **Schola Armaturarum** (Reg. IX, Ins. XX, no. 6). The doorway opening onto the street is almost as large as the room inside and is blocked by a wooden transenna which has been accurately reconstructed from the remains of the original. In one wall can be seen the slots into which fitted the cabinets which held weapons. All the decorations contain military motifs and on the divisions in the weapons cabinets are stylized chandeliers with the military symbols of the eagle and the globe. It is believed that this remarkable hall was occupied by a military association.

House of Trebius Valens: the outside triclinium with the unusual checkered polychrome decoration.

92 The HOUSE OF PINARIUS CERIALIS

(Reg. III, Ins. I, no. 6), further on past Via Nocerina, was the residence of a jewel worker (114 precious stones were found here, many of them already polished). It is a small dwelling, without an atrium, and on two sides has a very tiny portico. Extremely interesting is the Fourth Style decoration in the cubiculum to the left, depicting majestic theatrical figures and architectural features. In the large painting in the centre is Iphigenia in Tauris; in the two side paintings the figures of Venus, Attis and nymphs. The triclinium (behind and to the left of the peristyle) has some original and interesting decorations, as does the « oecus » used for the display and sale of merchandise.

House of the Moralist: the Winter Triclinium.

93 The House of the Moralist

(Ins. I, nos. 2-3) consists of connecting houses which belonged to two relatives, T. Arrius Polites and M. Epidius Hymenaeus. The house at no. 2 is the smaller one; its ceilings and decorations have been reconstructed and are especially interesting in the winter triclinium (at the back to the left). The wooden staircase leads to the upper floor where there are traces of decorations and small paintings such as those in the bedroom to the north, for example, depicting a satyr and a bacchant. The house on the right does not have an atrium although it does have a huge garden. The summer triclinium, looking onto the garden, has been uncovered complete together with the crockery used there. Standing out on the black background of its walls are three rules of etiquette written in white lettering which may be summed up as: (1) keep your feet clean and do not dirty the linen and beds; (2) have respect for women and avoid bad language; (3) refrain from anger and abuse and in conclusion, « aut gressus ad tua tectus refert » (otherwise go back to your own house).

94 The **HOUSE OF LOREIUS TIBURTINUS**

(Reg. II, Ins. II, no. 2) is a dwelling with an enormous garden and special features indicated, in this short summary, by the numbers used in the plan opposite.

The house (its ownership was attributed to Octavius Quartio by the discoverer, the architect, V. Spinazzola) belonged to a patrician Roman family. This much is clear from the two seats for waiting clients in the entrance and the monumental portal (1), which can be seen in a cast. Flanking the entrance are two rooms converted into shops (B) and connected to the house by a stair area. The large atrium (about 9 × 15 metres, or 29 ft × 48 ft), in which the decorations were never finished, had a marble impluvium adorned at one time with three fountains and surrounded by flower beds set in the floor (2). Traces of interesting paintings can be found in rooms (3) and (4); note the false windows opening onto imaginary gardens and the tondos with portraits of men and women. In the room to the left (5) is a small kiln for firing pottery. Next comes the pantry with a kitchen and small latrine (7).

Facing onto the peristyle with its hanging garden (8), after two « cubicula » (9) which have walls with a white and gold background, is the household shrine dedicated to the goddess Diana-Isis and decorated with the finest examples of paintings in the Fourth Style. On the facade of the shrine are, at left, Diana, and at right, Actaeon being torn to pieces by his hounds. On the inside is a lacunar or coffered ceiling, with box-like panels, which has been reconstructed from the original fragments; on the central wall is a niche for the gods; in the panel on the left is a probable portrait of the owner of the house, depicted as a prest of Isis, with below the inscription « amplus alumnus tiburs »; in the panel on the right is a painting depicting summer. In the « oecus tricliniaris » (11) are still visible traces of scenes from the Iliad and, at the top, scenes from the myth of Hercules.

The Upper Pergola (12) lying in front of the house, is full of statues and fountains and through the middle of it runs a canal (« euripus ») which was once teeming with fish. At the end of the pergola one can see the facilities for dining in the open, with two couches only at the sides of a fountain in a canopy-like structure (13); on the walls of the fountain are paintings of Pyramus and Thisbe on the right and Narcissus on the left; the artist who painted the pictures, a Roman, signed himself « Lucius pinxit ».

In the centre of the Upper Pergola is a small tetrastyle temple built over a nymphaeum and dedicated to Diana and Actaeon (14). The huge garden, on a slightly lower level than the house itself, was once a delightful place. In the centre can still be seen the long canal, which had innumerable fountains and was full of all types of fish, with statues and bas-reliefs along the sides. In the middle of the canal is a monumental fountain (15), followed by a small temple of the « euripus » (16), a pond and finally the exit from the garden with a small

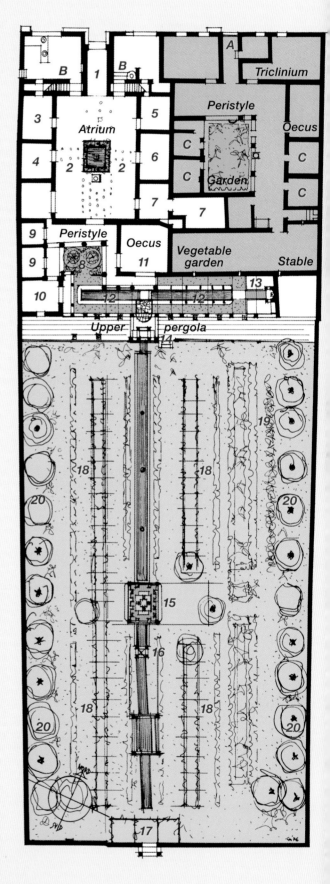

Facade of the House of Loreius Tiburtinus on Via dell'Abbondanza as it was before being destroyed in 79 A.D.. Notice the recess in the entrance with seats at the sides and the upper floor with two deep loggias (almost a reminder of the Propylaea in Athens). To the left can be seen the portal of the House of the Augustalis.

House of Loreius Tiburtinus. Above: upper pergola with transverse canal; left: fountain in a canopy-like structure with paintings on the walls.

« prothyron » (17). On the sides are many plaster casts of roots of climbing vines (18), plants with tall stems which bounded and shaded the large garden (19). To the left one can still see the vases (20) in which flowers were planted according to the seasons. The garden was thus a splendid area which transformed the house into a superb villa within the city walls.

In the plan as shown, the **House of the Augustalis** (Ins. II, no. 4) is indicated in grey to the right of the house of Loreius. On the handsome entrance portal (A), one can still see the Augustan emblem, which is a crown of oak between two laurel branches.

*House of Venus. Above: peristyle; right: Venus
on a seashell with cupids, depicted on the end wall
of the peristyle.*

95 The **HOUSE OF VENUS** (Ins. III, no. 3) was the house of a wealthy family which was being restored just before the tragic eruption. Damaged by the bombings in 1943, it was completely excavated and restored in 1952. In the room to the right of the atrium, note the fine paintings on a black backgrond and a portrait of a youth with a lyre. Three large paintings done with exquisite colours stand out on the back wall: three views of the blue sea seen with a garden hedge in the foreground. In the centre is Venus on a great seashell escorted by two Cupids; on the left is Mars and on the right are flowers and birds drinking from a fountain.

House of Julia Felix: garden with canal.

96 The **HOUSE OF JULIA FELIX** (Ins. IV, no. 3), already excavated and despoiled in 1755, was rediscovered in its entirety and much restored in 1952-1953. The house itself occupies a little more than one third of the entire block, one of the largest in Pompeii, and the rest is taken up by its orchard and garden.

The proprietress had fixed a notice to the entrance offering for rent two parts of the house: the superb private baths and the shops with living quarters (« venereum et tabernae »). The private bath area, in fact, was used only by important clients because it was « venereum », that is, worthy of a god. It had every possible facility: a portico used as a waiting room with seats, a cloak-room and a service-hatch from the nearby tavern; a dressing-room with tub for cold baths; a « tepidarium » near which was a « laconicum » (a vaulted circular area), forerunner to the modern sauna; a « calidarium »; and lastly, an area with open-air baths. The other part for rent consisted of rooms around the house: a tavern with triclinium and bedroom; shops with mezzanine (« pergulae ») and small living areas on the top floors (« cenaculae »).

The house itself has retained its atmosphere of patrician dignity despite the plundering done in the 18th century. Even today the garden is stately and impressive with its long fish-pond (« euripus »), the open-air triclinium in the centre of the eastern portico, and in particular the unusually beautiful western portico which has slender, elegant Corinthian pillars standing out against the decorations of the walls. There were were statues and fountains everywhere. The shrine on the south side was probably dedicated to the goddess Isis.

The last block on the right-hand side of Via dell'Abbondanza may have been occupied by the Forum Boarium or cattle market, or else by cages for the wild animals used in the games in the Amphitheatre. Recent excavations there have uncovered traces of a vineyard.

House of the Summer Triclinium. Above: the grandiose triclinium; right: one of the nymphaeums.

97 The zone to the south of Via dell'Abbondanza, including almost all of the First Region which extends from Porta Nuceria to Porta Stabia, is still being excavated. By actually seeing the work in progress, we can share that unforgettable feeling of discovering and restoring the remains of the ancient world. Among the excavations are projects undertaken by Japanese and American scholars (Ins. XVII).

Among other things in this zone, we can visit: the **House of the Summer Triclinium** (Reg. II, Ins. IX, no. 7), a grandiose triclinium in a garden which is especially interesting for its painted podium and two nearby nymphaeums with coloured mosaics; the **House of the Sarno Lararium** (Ins. XIV, no. 7), on the next block, with its small temple-lararium in which is a painting of a ship loaded with farm produce in the port of Pompeii (the Sarno River).

*Garden of the Fugitives: a startling view of plaster casts.
Thirteen human bodies were brought to light
in this area during the excavations undertaken
by the team of Giuseppe Ascione.*

The **Garum Workshop** (Ins. XII, no. 8) is also interesting as an example of a gastronomic industry which produced « garum », a sauce then in great demand, made from the entrails of fish fermented in sea water; the large containers and amphoras ready for shipping the product can still be seen. Opposite is the **House of the Ship Europa** (Reg. I, Ins. XV, no. 3), so called because of the « graffito » wall painting on the north wall of the peristyle depicting a ship and its life-boat with the inscription « Europa ». In the enormous garden, recent excavations led by Americans have uncovered the roots from a vegetable garden and orchard including such plants as legumes, onions, cabbages (much prized in an-

Partial view of the Necropolis of Porta Nuceria with various types of tombs brought to light by the last excavations.

cient times), cherries, peaches and lemons (used for medicines and deodorants). Next comes the **Thermopolium of the Phoenix** (Reg. I, Ins. XI, no. 10), a tavern with a large internal pergola which belonged to an Oriental named Euxinus. Its sign had a phoenix with two peacocks and the inviting inscription, « Phoenix: felix et tu », now in Naples. In the alley almost opposite is the **House of the Arches** (Reg. I, Ins. XVII, no. 4) where one of the rare arched porticoes in Pompeii can be seen.

During our tour, we will have seen many casts of bodies, but one of the most startling scenes testifying to the frightening tragedy of the people of Pompeii in 79 A.D. is the **Garden of the Fugitives** (Ins. XX, no. 5). It contains the casts of thirteen people, adults and children, a terror-stricken group who suffocated to death in the garden.

98 The **NECROPOLIS OF PORTA NUCERIA** is just outside the walls at the end of Via Nuceria. Recent excavations have already brought to light some interesting monuments, part of an outstanding monumental complex at the foot of the walls and the volcanic rock. In the southern part is the **Tomb of L. Ceius Serapius**, a banker, erected by his wife, Helvia.

On the eastern side note: a tomb with steps surmounted by an altar: the **Tomb of L. Cellius**, « tribunus », adorned with fine stucco panels. More chamber tombs follow, and then, on the other side of the street, comes the **Mausoleum of Veia Barchilla**, built for herself and « viro suo », meaning her husband, Agrestinus Equitius Pulcher. On the western side are a large tomb base, on which are writings to do with elections or announcements of

Necropolis of Porta Nuceria. Above: remains of the Mausoleum of the priestess Eumachia with the shrines of the married couple and of the Dignitaries at the sides; left: Porta Nuceria.

performances in the Amphitheatre (the two subjects of most interest to the Pompeians), and two sepulchres of freedmen with inscriptions and portraits. In the same area, below the walls of Pompeii, note the **Tomb of Eumachia**. It consists of a large, semi-circular monument with the inscription « Eumachia L(uci) f(ilia) sibi et suis », and the burial chamber at the back. To its left is a small temple with the tuff statues of a seated married couple; to the right, another small temple having an atrium with four columns which contains three tuff statues depicting two men wearing togas and a young man with his weapons, the inscription identifying it as the tomb of **M. Octavius and his wife Vertia Philumina**.

*The exedra-type mausoleum of the priestess
Eumachia as it was nineteen centuries ago.
The upper part has the same architectural motifs
as are on the large building erected by the priestess
in the Forum. At the ends are the two shrine-like
mausoleums with tuff statues in the pronaos:
on the left is the tomb of the seated married couple
and on the right that of the three standing dignitaries.*

Next come the **Sepulchre of the « gens Tillia »**, a family of important political figures, and the **tomb** in the form of an arch of the **freedman P. Vesonius Phileros**, a priest of Augustus, who at the end of his epitaph lays a curse on a treacherous friend.

Returning towards Porta Nuceria, on the right we come to the third major centre of Pompeii, this one dedicated exclusively to sports and the spectacles of the amphitheatre.

It is a grandiose complex which consists of two buildings only, the Amphitheatre and the Large Palaestra, but they occupy an area large enough to contain both the city's other two Forums together with all their buildings.

99 The **AMPHITHEATRE** was built in the year Pompeii became a Roman colony, 80 B.C., by the same magistrates who built the Small Theatre. It is of exceptional importance in that it is the oldest known amphitheatre. It measures about 135 by 104 metres (432 ft by 335 ft) and could hold 20,000 people. Unlike the Roman amphitheatres which were built later, the entrance ramps were all on the outside, there were no underground areas beneath the arena, and much of the arena was dug out to a level below that of the square outside the amphitheatre. The « ima cavea » (lower seating area) had five steps and was reserved for dignitaries; the « media cavea » and the « summa cavea » (middle and upper areas) had 12 and 18 steps respectively. The upper gallery, which was separated from the other areas and had its own stairs and entrances, was reserved for women (who were allowed to go to the amphitheatre thanks to a decree by the Emperor

Bird's eye view of the large Palaestra and the Amphitheatre, as they were one thousand nine hundred years ago. Following pages: the Amphitheatre.

Views of the exterior and interior of the Amphitheatre.

Augustus). Along the topmost part of the amphitheatre can still be seen the stone rings into which poles were inserted to hold up an enormous canopy. This was the « velarium », like the one used 100 years later in Rome's much larger Colosseum (188 by 156 metres or 602 ft by 489 ft), which protected spectators from sun and rain.

The amphitheatre was used exclusively for sports and gladiator contests, hunts and battles with wild animals. Introduced by the Romans, these spectacles became so popular that the amphitheatre soon had to be enlarged. People came from all the centres around Pompeii to the amphitheatre, and there was fierce rivalry among the towns. In fact, as Tacitus tells us in his « Annals », during a gladiators' contest in 59 A.D. a fight started between the men of Pompeii and those from the nearby Nuceria (now Nocera); it became so violent and left so many dead and wounded that the Roman Senate, on Nero's order, forbade all spectacles there for ten years.

Two views of the Large Palaestra.

100

The **LARGE PALAESTRA**, during the Imperial age, took the place of the Samnite one near the theatres, which was by this time too small for the city's needs. It was equipped for doing athletic exercises and for the annual exhibitions of the « Collegium Iuvenum ». It consisted of an enormous square (130 by 140 metres, or 448 by 416 ft) completely surrounded by a high wall with battlements and with entrances to the east and west; on the inside, along three sides, was a portico of Ionic columns. To the southeast is the latrine of considerable size. In the middle is a large swimming pool with the bottom sloping from west to east and steps on one side for entering the water; around the pool was a double row of tall plane-trees. A cryptogram (writing in cipher) was found on one of the columns in the westen portico, showing that there were probably Christians in Pompeii.

We can leave the Amphitheatre by the new entrance, and thus conclude our visit with this final impression of the great stadium where two thousand years ago the whole population of the city attended the « games » of those days with much the same enthusiasm and excitement seen in our own stadiums today. It is the end of our lengthy encounter with these people of Pompeii, visitors from two thousand years ago, and perhaps not so different from us as may first have appeared.

NEW POMPEII

Leaving the excavations by the Amphitheatre entrance, on the left is the beginning of the built-up area of new Pompeii. It is actually a small town occupying an area inhabited even after the famous eruption of 79 A.D. Called Campo Pompeiano, it has undergone many vicissitudes during the past centuries. A church dedicated to the Saviour was built there, as well as a castle which belonged to Caracciolo. The whole area was feudal territory which was passed from hand to hand, changing with the political situation of the Kingdom of Naples. In 1873 the lawyer Bartolo Longo (1841-1926), a religious and charitable man, founded the Sanctuary of the Madonna of the Rosary, around which he built, with the help of the faithful, charitable institutions and orphanages. The sanctuary soon became a centre of fervent worship. Many pilgrims from all over Italy flock here, especially in summer and autumn. The construction of the imposing sanctuary was begun by Antonio Cua in 1876. Consecrated on May 7, 1891, the sanctuary was enlarged in 1933-39 after a design of Spirito Chiappetta. On top of the façade stands the marble statue of the Madonna del Rosario by Gaetano Chiaramonte. The three-aisled interior is filled with precious marbles, frescoes and mosaics decorate the dome and the walls. In the middle is the main altar with the venerated image of the Virgin of the Rosary surrounded by myriads of precious stones. From the left-hand aisle one reaches the Treasury which vaunts many precious religious fittings as well as a St. Paul painted on wood, attributed to Fra Bartolomeo. It is worth while also to visit the belltower from the terrace of which one can enjoy a superb view.

Via Roma; below: monument to Bartolo Longo and detail. Following page: the exterior and interior of the imposing Shrine of Santa Maria del Rosario (Madonna of the Rosary).
Page 126: Bird's eye view of the excavation area.

INDEX OF SITES

Entries in **bold type** refer to the most interesting sites; numbers and letters in *italic type* serve to locate the site in the grid on the map provided separately with the volume. Numbers shown on the map refer to the numbered section in the volume describing the site.

SITES